Praise For

THE BOOK OF YES

"YES! The Book of YES is the modern bible for real estate success. Kevin Ward's brilliant, "No BS" scripts are the words agents need to 2X, 3X, 4X their business immediately. Stop! Don't go on an appointment without every word, sentence and paragraph memorized, rehearsed and ready for you to hear YES after YES."

- **Greg Hague,** Founder,
Real Estate Mavericks

"The Book of YES is a break-through book and a must-read for real estate agents. Kevin Ward understands the power of relationships and building true rapport with people."

- **Harvey Mackay,** author of the #1 New York Times bestseller
Swim With The Sharks Without Being Eaten Alive

"Average real estate agents fight using scripts. The pros seek out the ones that work the best and win! Kevin Ward's The Book of Yes is filled with scripts to help you win more listings. Get it. Read it. List more properties than ever before. Win!"

- **Tom Hopkins,** author of
Mastering the Art of Selling Real Estate

"Kevin Ward has created emmy winning scripts that will never appear on TV. They appear in person, on the phone, and in email performances...and the YES prize for winning is not a statue, It's a fatter wallet. More than just

The Book of YES, this one volume will lead you to the promised land of YES!"

- **Jeffrey Gitomer**, #1 bestselling author of
The Little Red Book of Selling

"Kevin has mastered how to use your voice and words to influence people and move them emotionally, and all the while being authentic and genuinely caring about the people you influence."

-**Roger Love,** The #1 Vocal Coach in America
Creator of Voice of Success

"I was Kevin's first broker and I saw how hard he worked to learn the business. I encouraged him to be a good listing agent so that he could not only control his income but so he could also control his time. The Book of Yes is absolutely fantastic. Every Real Estate agent should read and memorize the scripts that Kevin has put forth, whether they are experienced or brand new in the business. The Book of Yes can teach Realtors how they can control their business and not let their business control them."

- **Mike Bowman,** Founder & President of Century 21 Mike Bowman Inc.
#1 Century 21 Office in the World 18 times

"I have known Kevin for a long time and I can honestly say he has written a masterpiece in "The Book of YES." He articulately explains the importance of not only what to say, but the real reasoning behind the why. This is definitely a must read for anyone who truly wants to be a professional and have a successful career in real estate!"

- **Dave Bowman,** COO of Century 21 Mike Bowman Inc.
#1 Century 21 Office in the World 18 times

THE BOOK OF

YES

THE ULTIMATE REAL ESTATE AGENT CONVERSATION GUIDE

Kevin Ward

YESMasters, INC. edition 2016

Printed in the USA

ISBN-10: 1523610840

ISBN-13: 978-1523610846

Contents

Dedication

To Julie -

The girl of my dreams who finally said "Yes" to me,

my companion,

my partner,

my lover,

my inspiration,

and the one who will not tolerate even one ounce of B.S. in me.

Thank you, My Love.

How To Use This Book

The Book of "YES" is an *action guide*, not a book of theory. This is not a book to be read. This is a book to be studied and mastered...and most importantly this is a book to be used. Think of it as YOUR PLAY BOOK for the key conversations you have with sellers and buyers. Along with the scripts you will find tactical notes on how to use the script, why it works, and when to modify the script for various situations.

Because there are literally an infinite number of variables in any conversation with a prospect or client, there could theoretically be an endless number of scripts which would not be very practical. What I have done for you in **The Book of "YES"** is provide the most effective things to say in the most common scenarios that agents face in prospecting and in conversations and meetings with sellers and buyers.

Focus on Listings. My first broker, Mike Bowman, told me, *"Listings are the name of the game."* He was right. The reason is because taking salable listings is the path to a consistently profitable and sustainable real estate business that gives you time control (in other words not having to work 24/7) with the ability to do high levels of production (50, 100, 200 deals a year or more) while still having a life. Because of this, most of the scripts in this book focus on working with sellers rather than buyers. When you master inspiring sellers to say "yes" to you, you have found the magic key to being a successful real estate agent.

PART 1: The Art of "YES" gives you the foundation for making the scripts work effectively. Scripts are not natural for us, any more than playing the piano is natural. It has to be learned and approached as an art. Part 1 is 9 (short) chapters to give you the proper foundation for what I call the "Art of YesMastery," which is mastering the ability to inspire people to hire you and then to deliver the results for which they hired you.

Each chapter in Part 1 covers a key point for using scripts effectively or a key element of real estate success. DON'T skip these chapters. I know...I know, no one likes to "read the instructions." I don't either, but your improved effectiveness and results will be well worth the time to study the information in the first half of this book.

PART 2: The Words of "YES" contains the actual scripts, the choreographed conversations that make the "magic" happen.

Watch for the boxes that say "**YESMaster Strategy**." These are key training points usually relating directly to that script. Study and learn the *strategy*, because that will dramatically increase your understanding of how to say it *and* the psychology behind what the script is doing and why it should be said that way.

Part 2 is also laid out in a way to make it easy to find the script you need quickly (using the table of contents).

The first part is the Prospecting Scripts for sellers that lead up to the listing appointment.

Next is the Listing Presentation Script with notes on how to effectively deliver it. This also includes some objection handlers for getting the sellers to price it right and how to include your Guaranteed Sale if you offer one.

Third are the Buyer Scripts. This includes the "Buyer Sheet" which is the lead sheet you want to use with every buyer, because it also includes all the questions you want to ask to pre-qualify a buyer-lead for motivation, readiness, and ability to buy. This section also includes the "Open House Event Scripts" which are very important to help you get better results with buyers *and* with sellers who walk into one of your Open House Events.

Finally are the Objection Scripts. The objections are organized into Pre-Appointment Objection-Handlers (to be used before the listing presentation) and Listing Presentation Objection-Handlers (to be used only during the actual listing appointment). The reason this is important is because you want to handle as few objections as possible over the phone before you meet. *The secret to overcoming sellers' objections is to handle them only when you are sitting down with them at a listing presentation.* The only objections you want to handle over the phone are the ones you *have* to handle in order to get the appointment.

BONUS TRAINING RESOURCES. As my gift of appreciation to you for purchasing this book, and because I am committed to helping you succeed, I have provided for you a ton of additional training resources at no charge at www.thebookofyes.com/bonuses.

There you will find additional training videos teaching advanced communication skills and explaining in detail how to use these scripts. You will see me refer to specific videos on the bonus website throughout the book. Plus, you get complimentary letter-size pdf downloads of the scripts so you can print them and post them in your prospecting area or put them into a script binder.

My goal is to make this book so valuable and useful for you, that it becomes your "Ultimate Conversation Guide" for talking to prospects and clients, and leading to awesome results for you and your business.

INTRODUCTION

I wrote **The Book of "YES"** for two reasons.

Number one, ***because I hate B.S.***, and so many (if not most) real estate sales scripts are full of "B.S." (Bait-n-Switch, Bogus Statistics, Baloney Statements, etc.) If you have ever used scripts, then I'm sure you know what I'm talking about.

Here is the truth. *B.S. is the strategy of amateurs, not pros.* Frankly, people are tired of our B.S. ("bad sales") approaches. We can do better than that, and my goal is to give you the tools to have honest, straight-forward conversations with prospects and clients that will lead them to say "Yes," to you.

Number two, I started creating my own scripts, **because I *hated* being told**, **"No."** For me nothing was worse than that feeling of rejection. I was determined to figure out the perfect thing to say in every situation, and how to say it in a way that would cause sellers and buyers to *want* to say "Yes!" to me. This book is the result of that quest over the last 17 years full-time as a real estate agent, broker, trainer, and coach.

I believe *these are the best and most powerful scripts ever written for real estate agents.*

"That's pretty big talk, Kevin. How can you say that?"

Why I can say these scripts are the BEST:

First because of <u>**experience:**</u> The scripts in this book are the result of over 17 years in the trenches almost every day actually talking to sellers and buyers or coaching and training other agents. I have put in thousands of hours prospecting, including the toughest prospects out there: expired listings, for-sale-by-owners, and "cold-calling." (The very thought of "cold-calling" still makes me shiver with dread.)

I have been told "*no*" thousands and thousands of times. Experimenting and practicing on sellers and with other agents. Studying every script that I could get my hands on. Writing and re-writing. Creating my own scripts. Editing. Tweaking. I've tried countless variations. Always looking for the ideal question. The perfect word. The magic phrase. The exact technique or pause.

And because I was willing to put in the work, I've had thousands and thousands of "Yes's" talking to sellers and buyers, and listing and selling houses. And I have now coached and trained thousands of real estate agents all over the world, and have seen their results using these scripts. I have witnessed dramatic increases in the number and quality of appointments set and listings taken once agents begin using and mastering the scripts you hold in your hand.

Second, because of **expertise** (which is different than experience). For over 25 years, I have studied communication skills and influence and persuasion strategies. I have studied language and words. I have explored and sought to understand the energy and connotations of the words and phrases we use. I have discovered the words and phrases commonly used by real estate agents that automatically cause sellers and buyers to unconsciously (and sometimes consciously) resist them. These are "*resistance triggers.*" I learned to eliminate them, and immediately the results improved. Next, I have researched and identified "*influence triggers*" (words and phrases) that cause people to *want* to hire you.

And third, because of **my "B.S. Detector."** I have a highly-trained knack for sniffing out B.S. and then simply eliminating all the B.S. I flushed it out of the scripts. If you have ever read or used a script that made you feel like you were trying to "con" or "B.S." someone, this is the answer you have been waiting for. *You can get "yes" without the B.S.* Your prospects and clients don't want it. And you don't need it.

You may be asking yourself right now, "Do I really need more scripts?" You may be feeling like, "I don't even like scripts." I totally get it. I felt the same way when I started selling real estate. I did not want to sound like a telemarketer or high-pressure solicitor. Don't worry. This book will help you realize that you don't have to be any of that.

So…CONGRATULATIONS for picking up a book of scripts! Whatever possessed you to give **The Book of "YES"** a serious look…you will be glad you did.

And…after you've read it, if you don't agree the scripts are the best you have ever used, I will gladly give you a full refund for the book and any shipping and handling you paid for it. Simply send an email to support@YESMasters.com.

Oh yes…I put my money where my mouth is…because *I want you to succeed more than I want to sell you a book.* And if this book helps you succeed, please let me know about it at Kevin@YESMasters.com and help me spread the word. Your successes inspire and motivate me and others. You win. And we all win. YES!!!

Part -1

THE ART OF YES

Chapter 1

MASTERY: WHY IT MATTERS

When you master the art of inspiring people to say "yes" to you and then delivering great results for them, you open the door for yourself to true abundance and success and having the life of your dreams. I believe that is the ultimate "Yes," being able to say "yes" to your goals and dreams and to your family and their dreams.

That is my real passion, helping you create the lifestyle you want. I believe agents don't get into real estate just to sell a lot of houses. We got into real estate to *have a LIFE.* We all believed at some level that having our own real estate business would give us greater control over our time and our income, and ultimately more control over our lives.

Look, if you're selling a ton of houses, but you're working 24/7 and never able to take a real vacation…or you're missing all your kids' soccer games…that sucks. That's not success for most people. My commitment is to help you make more money, add more value, and have a life. When you are winning in all three of those areas, you are a YesMaster.

Chapter

2

DISTINCTIONS: MORE SCRIPTS?

Occasionally someone says, "Kevin, your scripts sound just like all the others..." or "All the scripts sound pretty much the same..." And it is true that most scripts for real estate agents *appear* to be pretty similar. But...don't miss this...*it's the differences that matter,* and as you study and begin to use the scripts and strategies in this book, *you* will begin to notice the distinctions and the power of the differences.

A couple of years ago I was in Hawaii and decided to buy a ukulele. On the Island of Oahu in a small village, right next to the narrow two lane highway on the north side of the island from Honolulu, there is a little shop that is one of the most renowned ukulele stores in the world. When we walked in, we were greeted with walls that were covered with ukuleles hanging there for sale.

All the ukuleles looked pretty much the same to me...until I started looking at the prices. One for $59. Another for $159. Oh...and there's one for $759! Are you kidding me?! I couldn't believe the price differences. There were dozens of these "mini-guitars" that were actually selling for *thousands* of dollars! And for the next half hour a ukulele expert educated me and demonstrated for me the "slight differences" that made huge differences. Some were imported hard woods. Others were laminates. Some were machine made, while the good ones were made by hand. All of these factors had a major impact on the sound quality and the value. Yes…it's the differences that matter.

It is the same with cars. At a distance a Dodge can look a lot like a Bentley, but it's the *differences* that make one a $40,000 car and the other a $240,000 car.

In **The Book of "YES"**, you will not only find the most powerful scripts in the real estate industry, you will also learn what makes a script powerful, as well as the distinctions…the seemingly little differences that actually make a huge difference in the way a prospect or client responds to what you say. Learn to recognize the *differences*, and you will dramatically increase the number of leads, appointments, listings, and sales you will generate.

Chapter 3

PROS ONLY: AMATEURS NOT ALLOWED

Before we go any further I want to clarify something that might save you a lot of time. *Scripts are for pros only.* They're not for amateurs. If you're looking for some magic bullets that will instantly demolish every objection you face, this book will not save you. A script used by an amateur *sounds* like a script being used by an amateur, and it is a *big* turn off.

When you attend one of my 3-day live training camps, you will see a sign that says: "PROS ONLY. AMATEURS NOT ALLOWED." I used to try to figure out why no one wanted to attend role play to work on mastering scripts and communication skills. One day it finally occurred to me that we are basically an industry of amateurs. I know that statement may offend some people, but it's true.

Let me explain it this way. When I was taking piano lessons in 3rd grade, my piano teacher told me I was not going to be allowed to play in the Winter Recital. Why? Because I was supposed to practice 30 minutes a day…and I wouldn't do it. My teacher knew that if he let me play in the recital, I would embarrass my parents, myself, and him, so he said, "no."

Compare that to the amount of time a professional concert pianist practices every day. Six to eight hours! What about the Olympic athlete? How many hours a day do they spend practicing and preparing for their performance?

In Oakland, basketball fans will show up two hours before a Golden State Warriors game starts just to watch NBA MVP Stephan Curry's *practice!* Why? Because virtually nobody has ever been able to shoot and handle the ball like Curry. Why? Because no one practices as much as Steph Curry. That's why the Warriors are the NBA Champions.

Now, compare all of that to the amount of time the average *agent* spends each day practicing what to say and how to say it when talking to prospects and clients…which is on average exactly zero minutes per day! Do you realize that your ability to talk and communicate effectively with people is the single most important skill you have for making money?

When you go on a listing appointment, you are literally auditioning for a $5,000, $10,000, or even $20,000 commission check or more, representing the sale of a client's most valuable asset in the world, and yet the average agent spends less time per day practicing their listing presentation skills than a 9-year-old spends preparing to play one song in a piano recital. Are you kidding me?

Amateurs are the ones who are always looking for a shortcut…a "tip" that will catapult them to get more listings. They want the results without the price.

Pros don't look for "tips." Tips are f
looking for an easy path to success. There is
is mastery and there is mediocrity. They are
never found on the same path. The path
learning tips and tricks, but in mastering ski
are only available to the committed.

Having a real estate license or a business card or a website or even a "designation" does not make you a pro in real estate, any more than having a basketball and a pair of Nikes makes you a pro in basketball. If you are not willing to do the work to go pro and invest the time to learn and practice and master what to say and how to say it, don't waste your time reading this book. But I have a feeling if you've made it this far…you're ready to go pro. So let's go!

Chapter

4

TECHNIQUE: WHAT YOU NEED TO KNOW

TRIGGER WORDS AND PHRASES

"Triggers" are words and phrases that we say that tend to create a certain emotional response or association for people. For example, "NO," is a very strong "resistance trigger," which means people will automatically resist you when you tell them "no." Why? Because ever since you were a little child, "no" represented restriction. It meant you could not have or do something you wanted.

You will learn to recognize and eliminate the "RESISTANCE TRIGGERS" that are in almost every traditional real estate sales script. Resistance triggers are words and phrases that make people resist you. You will also discover the power of "INFLUENCE TRIGGERS," the words and phrases that cause people to lower their resistance and to want to say "YES" to you.

THE POWER OF TIE-DOWNS

As you read the scripts, you will notice "tie-downs." A tie-down is a simple, short question that is tagged onto a statement, that is designed to cause a response from the listener. For example, "You do want to get top dollar for your property, right?"

The word "right?" is a tie down. There are simple tie downs such as "…, right?" or "…, correct?" or "…, isn't it?"

And then there are influence tie-downs that create the feeling of collaboration, such as "*…are you with me?*" When you ask that question after making an important statement, and they answer, "yes," (which they will do), subconsciously you just created synergy. You just got on their side! It's almost magical. Watch for the variety of tie-downs used in the scripts, especially in the listing presentation.

Tie-downs are very important also for keeping the seller engaged in the conversation. When you are just telling them information, sellers attention span can be alarmingly short. Asking questions, which a tie-down does, keeps the client actively involved and engaged in the conversation. The feedback you get from these tie-downs also tells you something about how well the seller is getting what you are saying.

EMBEDDED COMMANDS

An "embedded command" is an NLP influence strategy of inserting a verbal command into a question or statement so that it communicates a call to action without coming across as demanding or as an explicit command at all. This is because the command is essentially hidden inside a simple question or statement. Here is an example of an embedded command from the beginning of The Listing Presentation Script:

"Are you definitely ready to... sell your property?" The command is "sell your property." However, it is inserted or "embedded" inside of a question. The bottom-line effect is that you are asking a relevant question that keeps them involved in the conversation, that gives you important information about their motivation, and that is simultaneously encouraging them to take action.

Do not feel like you are being manipulative using this technique. If you are meeting with someone who actually has a need or desire to sell their property, you are simply encouraging them to take action or make a decision that is in *their best interest.*

Technique is not manipulative. If someone's motivation is self-serving or exploitive, then using "technique" can be very manipulative. When you care about the clients' best interest and you genuinely want to help them, then learning influence skills and techniques is actually very respectful. It means that you care enough about them and about being effective, that you are willing to approach your professional relationship with them with skill. Leading people to make a good decision that is good for them is a good thing, not a bad thing.

See my BONUS training video on "Embedded Commands" at www.thebookofyes.com/bonuses.

IMPORTANT NOTE: In the scripts, embedded commands are set apart by ". . ." (3 dots) and are . . . in *larger print* to remind you to . . . use the embedded commands. The ". . ." also reminds you to pause . . . which is extremely important to . . . give your words power . . . that will inspire people to say "YES" to you.

Chapter 5

PRACTICE: THE SECRET OF THE BEST

In Hollywood there is a saying among actors: "The script is the enemy." That does not mean that actors do not like or do not use scripts. Scripts are a part of the business. The enemy is when it *sounds like* you are performing from a script. The cardinal sin of acting is to sound unnatural playing the part. As long as it sounds like you are reading a script, the script is your enemy.

Once the actor so internalizes the script and embodies the character they are playing so completely that they essentially "become" the person...that's when the script is no longer the enemy. The best actors and actresses in the world are the ones who relentlessly practice, and study, and rehearse to *become* the part they are playing.

I like to refer to what I teach as **conversational choreography**, rather than mechanical "scripts and dialogues." It's like a professional figure skater. Their routine or program in its basic, stripped down version is a skating "script"...a triple lutz followed by a double axel...and so forth. However, when it is performed with skill that comes from practicing and rehearsing over and over again, it becomes a graceful, artistic performance that is fluid, powerful, and almost effortless. And the amazing thing is, it looks totally natural.

The best Olympic skaters know that the *real work* is not performing. The real work is *practicing.* That's where the gold medal is won. Not under the lights, in front of the crowds, in a custom-made, sparkling dance costume; but on a practice rink without the lights, with no crowds or cheers, and in plain leotards and sweats. Practice. Rehearse. Wipe out. Get up. Dust off. Do it again. And again. Practice. One more time. And over. And over. And over...until muscle memory takes over and the skater can move through the entire routine almost without thought.

My hero has always been Michael Jordan. Michael is the greatest basketball player of all time, not because he was the most talented, but because no one else practiced and trained as intensely or as much as he did. In his own words, "nobody else has wanted it as bad as I wanted it. No one else has been willing to put in the hours." His attitude is, "you may not like the hard work, but you will love the results."

The secret of the world's most elite performers is how they approach practice. The elite figure skater is committed to perfecting both the technical elements of each move as well as the artistic presentation of the routine. When it is all combined into their final skating program, it is a powerful expression of their skill and grace. It's automatic. Flawless. Powerful. Breathtaking. It is all the result of countless hours of practice and rehearsal. There may not be any glamour on the practice rink, but without it, there will be no gold medal. That is the real work of elite performers in any sport or industry.

The concert pianist, the extreme big-air snow-boarder, the professional golfer, the Broadway actress, the real estate agent. They all have one core thing in common…their success is directly tied to the level of their performance. The better your communication skills are when you speak to a prospect, the better results you are going to get. The more skill and confidence you have when handling an objection, the more appointments and listings you will have. This is a win for you *and* a win for each and every client.

Chapter 6

CONFIDENCE: THE ONE QUESTION

When a seller is considering you as their agent, they have *one unspoken question* that they most want answered:

"Are you the best agent to help me get the best results?"

The moment they believe the answer to that question regarding you is "Yes," their answer *to* you will be "Yes." What sellers want and need is *confidence.* They want to feel certain that you are the right agent. What they do *not* want is to get stuck with a bad agent.

The question is, where do sellers get this confidence?

Answer: they get it best and most powerfully from *you.*

If you are confident, they *feel* it. If you are able to respond to their questions and objections with certainty, they feel that. You are relaxed. You are sure. You're comfortable handling their curveball objections. They may or may not like your answers, but they feel safe in the fact that you know your stuff.

Everything you do and say communicates to them, "I got this." Confidence. BOOM! Game over. The listing is yours.

Chapter 7

INFLUENCE: BEYOND THE SCRIPT

Mastery goes beyond the scripts and beyond the mechanical techniques of traditional "sales closes" and NLP (Neuro-Linguistic Programming) techniques. While the conversations in this book are indeed scripted, I want you to understand what makes a script dynamic and powerful is much more than just the words. The goal is influence. To have real influence, words matter, *and* how you say the words matters even more.

A script is like a musical instrument or a golf club or tennis racquet. It is only as effective as your ability to skillfully perform with it. *The quality of the instrument becomes more important as the skill level of the one using it increases.*

Think of it as three magical keys that will unlock the power of scripts and open the door to more "yes's":

#1. Learning what to say. This is the simple process of learning the scripts; learning the right things to say and the right questions to ask at the right time. Also you want to know what *not* to say, which I will also help you learn.

#2, Learning *how* to say it. As you learn what to say, you are also mastering the delivery of *how* you say it, so that it comes across to your prospect as authentic and conversational.

#3. Learning how to *listen*. This is why it is critical that you *internalize* the scripts, so they become *automatic*. When you are worried what you are going to say next, you can't focus on listening to the client. You're stuck in your own head, and they can usually tell it. Once you master the "choreographed conversations," now you can engage better with the client and actually *hear* how they are responding, so you know better how to respond.

Don't worry if all this sounds like a lot to absorb. Mastery is a journey. It is not going to happen overnight, but it will happen for you. That is also why I created the BONUS companion video training for you at www.thebookofyes.com/bonuses, where we actually dive into the nitty gritty techniques and processes of mastering these conversations that are key to your real estate success.

I remember the first time I picked up a golf club and tried to hit the ball with it. It was amazing how tiny the ball seemed sitting there. I wound up and swung, and whoosh…I got nothing but air! The ball didn't even move. Over the next two hours as I played my first round of golf, the ball went just about every direction I didn't want it to go. Most of the time (except when I was putting) I felt lucky if I even hit the ball at all! It would not have mattered if I was using an old worn-out club or a custom high-dollar professional driver. I was awkward and out-of-control. Why? Because I didn't know how to swing it! But put the same club in the hands of a professional golfer, and they can knock the ball straight down the fairway over 300 yards. What's the difference? Skill gained from countless hours of training and practice.

A powerful script is a planned conversation that allows you to connect with your prospect or client and lead them to a decision without BS-ing them. That is *influence.*

Scripts are not magical incantations that when you read them will automatically cause sellers to give you an appointment or a listing, just as picking up a top-of-the-line golf club does not make you instantly a fabulous golfer. A quality golf club will make a ton of difference, but only in the hands of someone skilled in its use. The same with a script.

The purpose of a script is not to manipulate people against their will. "Handling objections" is not to "beat the seller into submission" or to "out-talk" them. It is to honestly address the questions and concerns that a client or prospect have and do it in a way that gives them the confidence they need to have in you. This will cause them to willingly and confidently say "Yes" to you as their agent. That is leadership. That is influence.

However, I believe the real power to inspire people to say "yes" to you goes even beyond skill. It goes to the heart.

Chapter

8

HEART: YOU GOTTA HAVE IT

While I teach and emphasize the skilled use of scripts and proven techniques, I start with a fundamental pre-supposition that makes all the difference. And that is that *It's all about the client! It's not about me.*

Your responsibility as a professional agent is to *add value to the client,* not to take advantage of them. Your job is not to take listings. *Your job is to deliver results for the clients who hire you.* I am not at all comfortable when I see real estate agents who are trying to learn "seduction" strategies taught by pick-up artists. They tend to be highly manipulative and totally self-serving. The *"wham, bam, thank you ma'am"* approach to real estate sales is empty and poison because it is exploitative and serves no one's best interest in the long run.

When your highest interest is the client's best interest…*now* you have true power. At the heart of this is that you must be genuine in your commitment to doing what is best for them. This is not a "technique." It is a value system. It is *heart.* It is character.

…s long as a prospect thinks you are only after a listing or a …eck, they are going to resist you like crazy. When a seller or …yer believes you know what you are doing *and* they perceive that you care, they feel *safe.* When they feel safe, they say "yes."

There is a huge difference between trying to *sound* interested in their situation and genuinely *being* interested. True mastery is not about how you *sound,* but about how you *are.* Sounding interested, which can indeed be a learned skill, must grow out of you actually being interested. All other things being equal, skill with "heart" will win over skill with "technique" alone every single time. *Yes*…what's in your heart matters.

Chapter 9

COLLABORATION: THE ULTIMATE RAPPORT

What makes a script really powerful is that your *intention* is to find out what is most important to the Seller or Buyer. In other words, what is *their* motivation? Then you can use these choreographed conversations that will lead them to make decisions that accomplish *their* motivation…not just yours. The result is that they feel and know that you are on their side.

The ultimate rapport is collaboration…working together to achieve a common goal. When they sense that level of connection with you, all their resistance melts away.

When you grasp the power of these three elements: ***heart***, ***skill***, and ***confidence,*** then you are ready for what this book can really help you accomplish! When you master that level of heart, combined with mastery of skill and complete confidence, ***people will not be able to say "no" to you.***

Chapter

10

NINE KEYS TO MORE POWERFUL CONVERSATIONS

1. **Stand up.** When you are talking to prospects on the phone, your energy level is higher and your voice comes across much more powerfully when you are standing. When you're practicing and role-playing, always be on your feet. Virtually the only time you want to be sitting is during the actual listing presentation...and even then you want to be "*standing*" mentally. An agent who comes across as laid back or low energy does not inspire a seller or a buyer. They want a go-getter. On your feet. Eager. Ready.

2. **Smile big**. First impressions last forever. A genuine smile is the most powerful tool you have to connect with someone quickly and naturally. Even on the phone, people can literally hear a smile. A *smile* communicates, "I like you, and I like what I'm doing." People instinctively know that you will do a better job when you actually enjoy it, so look

like you're enjoying it. When you're smiling, you're delivering happiness, and they feel it.

3. **Speak with confidence**. The most important thing for a seller to feel from you *and* about you is confidence. This is more than trusting that you are honest. They need to trust that you are competent, that you can deliver results. When you speak, you want your words and tonality to communicate certainty. This means speaking with a pleasant yet assumptive tone. When you have that confidence, it is easy for them to feel it. That's when they hire you!

   A very powerful NLP (Neuro-Linguistic Programming) technique that communicates confidence is a *downswing*. A downswing is when you finish a question or statement with your tone-of-voice going down, rather than your tone going up as we do when we ask a question. An "*upswing*" tends to communicate that we are uncertain. For a BONUS video with examples of how to use downswings effectively go to www.thebookofyes.com/bonuses

4. **Be energetic and enthusiastic**. Clients want to know that you *want* to help them. If you sound bored or uninterested or even worse, inconvenienced, it is difficult to get them to trust you. They need to know that you are excited about what you are doing because we instinctively know that people give more effort and perform better when they are doing something they enjoy. In fact, enthusiasm gives anyone an immediate edge over other agents and can be used as effectively by a new agent as by a seasoned top-producer.

5. **Be conversational.** If you sound like you are following a script, you will not come across as authentic. Mastery is when you use the script as a strategically choreographed conversation in a way that *sounds* totally natural and spontaneous. The script insures you are saying the right things and asking the right questions to lead the prospect or client to a good decision. The key here is to internalize the scripts to the point that you don't have to think about what you are going to say next, because it is automatic. This allows you to focus your attention on *listening to the client*, rather than focusing on what you are going to say next.

6. **Be interested**. Be excited about what they are excited about! Be genuinely interested in their move and let it show in your conversation with them. Being interested implies caring. They know that someone who cares will do a much better job. This is more than *saying*, "I'm curious…" You want to actually *be* curious…be interested. Add to that an authentic desire to help them get the result they want, and you become unstoppable.

7. **Repeat and affirm**. As you go through the scripts, you will notice that after many of the questions, there are paragraph brackets like this: (   ), followed by an affirming response such as "Great!" "Fantastic!" "Good for you!" etc. In addition to the affirming word, you also want to *repeat* back to them their answer. If it's a longer or complex answer, you want to repeat back to them the gist of their answer or the most relevant part of their answer. I call this an "affirming echo," because you are echoing back to your prospect what you are hearing them communicate. You are *repeating* and *affirming* their answer to you.

When you repeat or reflect back another person's answer to a question, it does several very important things. First, it tells the client that you are listening to what they are saying and that it matters to you. Second, it forces you to actually pay attention to what they are saying, which helps you understand their motivation. *This is the most powerful rapport-building technique you can use.* It also creates a natural bridge from your last question to the next question. Repeating does not mean parroting their answer word for word. It means reflecting back to them the gist of their statement or response.

8. **Mirror and match**. Mirroring and matching is responding to people by matching their body language, tone, speed, volume, and even their emotion. People like people who are like them. A simple example is the speed with which we talk. If someone walks in and starts speaking much faster than you, there is a natural tendency to distrust them. We even use the term "fast-talker" to refer to a con-artist, someone who is not trustworthy. On the other hand, if a person speaks much slower than your natural pace, we tend to perceive that person as less intelligent. They talk slowly, so they must be "slow." When your pace matches the other person, they automatically resonate with you because you both have the same tempo. You "mirror and match" them.

9. **Practice! Practice! Practice!** Someone once asked a New York taxi cab driver, "How do you get to Carnegie Hall?" His simple answer was, "Practice. Practice. Practice." This is the real work of mastery. Professional athletes and performing artists are people - like real estate agents - whose results are directly tied to the level of their performance. They spend countless hours, weeks, and

years, practicing and rehearsing so that when they step into their arena, they can deliver a winning performance.

For you, a winning performance is one that gets an appointment or a salable listing. There is no short-cut. The more you internalize the scripts and practice using them in "choreographed conversations," the more confidence you will have and the more effective you will be. More practice equals more skill. More skill equals more confidence. And more confidence equals more "Yes's!"

If you will set aside one hour a day to practice, rehearse, and role play the scripts in this book, one year from now, your skill-level and confidence-level will be unrecognizable and you will be unstoppable

For a BONUS video I did years ago on these "9 Keys to More Powerful Conversations", go to www.thebookofyes.com/bonuses.

Part -2

THE WORDS OF YES

PROSPECTING SCRIPTS

PERSONAL CIRCLE®
(PC) SCRIPT

For use with Past Clients and Sphere of Influence

1. Hi, _______. This is ____________ at ________... How are you....?* ( ) Great!

2. ____________, the reason I'm calling today is because...I need your help! ...Do you have a quick minute? (Sure!) Great!

3. *I've set a goal to help at least _______ people in the next 90 days**...who are either going to be buying, selling, or investing in real estate...and...

> OR There are some tremendous opportunities right now...in the real estate market... [insert current information of value if available]...and...

4. I was wondering...who you've talked to recently that's looking to...buy a home,... sell a property, or...invest in real estate...in the next month or so...that I can help? ( ) I appreciate you thinking about it...

5. Have you bumped into anyone at work? ...or in your neighborhood? ...any family members? ...or at church [*etc.*]...that might need my help? Fantastic!

6. What would be the best way for me to get in touch with them?*** ( ) Awesome! Thank you!
7. I will give them a quick call...and introduce myself to them...and see what I can do to help! Is there anyone else you can think of? ( ) Excellent!
8. So...when do you think you might be ready to...make a move...or...invest in real estate? ( ) Good for you!

---

*[*OPTIONAL PERSONAL CIRCLE ICEBREAKER…if you have not talked to them in a while]:* "I was just thinking about you…in fact I've been meaning to call you…and I decided…today…I was just going to pick up the phone and actually call you...so how are things going?"

**[OR] - in the next 90 days/this summer/etc [pick a specific time frame]

****[OPTIONAL ADD]* …And you know I will take great care of them---because I want both you and them to…be glad you referred me to them. So, what's the best number for me to reach them? ( ) Perfect!

[HOW TO INTERRUPT a talkative person]: Hey, ______. I'm so sorry to have to do this. I've got an appointment**** I have to run right now. I'm so excited to hear more about ______. Why don't you give me a call some evening in the next week or two...and let's catch up? (Sure.) Great! Thanks.

****[*Your appointment is to stay on your prospecting schedule. Also, put the responsibility on them to call you, rather than tell them you will call them back.*]

YESMaster Strategy: *Learn and use the scripts word-for-word.* Every word and phrase in every script has a reason for being there the way that it is. Mastery always starts with the fundamentals. As my basketball coach used to say, *"Don't try the fancy stuff until you master the fundamentals!"* Resist the urge to "edit" the scripts to feel more "natural." I get it…I really do. But I challenge you to trust the process of mastery and trust that these conversations are tested and proven, and will work best when you master delivering them unaltered.

As a simple example, when you change the script from, "Who have you talked to recently…? to, "Do you know anyone…?" you completely change the quality of the response you will get. The second question feels more natural for a lot of people, but it sends a different request to the other person's brain (yes or no) that automatically kicks out a default "No" answer. That is *not* the answer you're going for, *so stick with the script.*

Personal Circle Script Modification For A New Agent:

1. Hi, _______. This is ____________... How are you....?*
   ( ) Great!

2. ____________, the reason I'm calling today is because...I need your help! ...Do you have a quick minute? (Sure!) Great!

3. In case you haven't already heard, I recently launched my career in real estate! Yeah...I'm very excited about it! And...I've set a goal to help at least _______ people in the next 3 months**...who are either going to be buying, selling, or investing in real estate....and...

[*Continue with #4 on the* PERSONAL CIRCLE SCRIPT]

FOR NEW AGENTS: The fastest way to get business as a newbie is to get the word out. Do not be a "secret agent" and say to yourself, "Once I prove myself on strangers, then I'll approach people I know." That approach is based on a *fear of failure* and the longer you wait, that fear becomes harder to overcome, not easier. You want to start leveraging your relationships immediately.

When you are a new agent, people you know will take their cue from you based on the level of enthusiasm and confidence you communicate. When you come across as excited and sure of yourself, they will feel comfortable using you and referring people to you.

If you know people who you expect may respond negatively, it is better to get it over with. It may be uncomfortable, but *your success in real estate will require you spending a lot of time outside your comfort zone.* Period. Bite the bullet. Make the announcement, ask for their support, and get ready to be surprised at the number of them who *will* give you business! Either way, just by taking the action and overcoming your own fear and internal resistance, YOU WIN!

For a bonus training video on "How to Overcome the Objection of Being a New or Young Realtor®", go to www.thebookofyes.com/bonuses

Personal Circle Objection-Handler:

> OBJECTION: *"Let me talk to them first before I give you their phone number."*

Absolutely! And I appreciate so much your willingness to… make that introduction! So let's do this. If you'll …give them a call …and …make the introduction...let me…go ahead… and get his/her number from you... now.

And then I'll wait to hear from you. After you talk to him/her, just …shoot me a quick text message …and …give me the green light. Then I'll give them a quick call...and all I'm going to do is touch base with them, introduce myself, and see if there's anything I can do to help. Fair enough? (Yes.) Perfect.

What is their number? (   ) Excellent. Thank you!

THE EXPIRED SCRIPT

Hi, is this _______________? Hi, _______________. My name is _______________. I'm a local real estate agent....and I was calling about your house for sale... I guess you're aware by now that the MLS is showing your home is "OFF" the market...

1. And I was wondering...when are you going to...interview agents again...for the job of actually getting it SOLD.... ( ) Excellent!/Really!
2. If your property had sold...where were you planning to go next? ( ) That's exciting!
3. What's taking you to _______________? ( ) Good for you!
4. How soon did you want to be there? ( ) Wow!
5. So ____________...any idea what stopped it from selling? ( ) Really!
6. How did you choose the last agent you had? ( ) That makes sense.
7. How did you feel about the job the agent did? ( ) That's good./Oh no!
8. So...what do you think was missing...that kept it from actually selling? ( ) Ooh!
9. Now...it sounds like...you do still...want to sell your property....right? (Yes.) Great!

10. If you could…get it sold…for top dollar…in the next 30 days… and… get ________________ [their motivation]…. That is something you would still...be excited about…yes? (Yes.) Perfect!

11. And...If I could help you…make it happen…that would be okay with you…right? (Right.) Excellent!

12. When would be the best time for us to...get together...and take a look at how we can make that happen...how about Wednesday at 4:15...or would Thursday at 4:15 be better?

YESMaster Strategy: When you introduce yourself to an Expired, it is best *not* to tell them what company you are with because it is much more likely to work against you than for you. If you're with a major name brokerage and they have any negative association with that brand, you just became the enemy when you announce your company. If there are other agents from your same company calling, you just become one of the crowd when you give your company name. If you are with a small brokerage, they may say, "I've never heard of you before," which obviously does not gain you any credibility. The fact that you are local is enough, and if you sell homes in their area, you *are* local.

MOTIVATION: If you have clear, strong motivation after #4, including *where*, *when*, and *why* they are moving, you can skip #5 through #8 and go straight to #9.

YESMaster Strategy: The power of *embedded commands* (which are indicated in the scripts by the larger font size and "…") is not force…in other words being louder or harder with your voice. That is what some trainers incorrectly teach. Raising your volume and making your tone demanding may be mechanically correct as an embedded command, but it is not as effective, because it can also sound pushy which simply creates additional resistance.

Done correctly, it is the inherent power of the confidence and certainty you have that inspires them to have that same confidence and certainty about hiring you. You want your embedded commands to sound inviting, not "gun-to-the-head" threatening.

Think of it as the way you might say to a friend, "Hey…would you like to…go shopping with me?" Now, just pretend like you are telling them in a very pleasant, suggestive tone, "Go shopping with me." That is a command, but it is inviting, not harsh or threatening or pushy.

You can check out my BONUS training video on "Embedded Commands" where I actually demonstrate the right way to do this at www.thebookofyes.com/bonuses.

Leaving A Voice Mail For An Expired:

Hi...this is ________. I'm a local real estate agent...and I was calling about your property for sale. The MLS is showing that it is now "OFF" the market. If you are still interested in selling, would you call me at ______________. [Repeat #]

Calling Old Expireds Script:

Hi, is this ______________? Hi, ______________...my name is ______________. I'm a local real estate agent....and I noticed that you had your house for sale...____________ [e.g. last year]....

1. And I was wondering...when are you planning to...put it back on the market...and actually...get it SOLD.... ( ) Excellent!/Really!

[*CONTINUE with #2 on the EXPIRED SCRIPT.*]

Door-knocking Expired Script:

[When door-knocking, you simply modify the script to the following:]

Hi, are you ______________? (Yes.) My name is ______________. I'm a local real estate agent....and I was dropping by to find out about your house for sale... I guess you're aware by now that the MLS is showing your home is "OFF" the market...

[Then proceed with #1 on the EXPIRED SCRIPT above.]

Working with Expired and Cancelled Listings

Expireds are a constant flow of *free listing leads*, and they are a *gold mine* if you are willing to master the game of Expired Listings. The approach for expired listings and for cancelled listings is virtually the same. Listing agreements that are cancelled or expired indicate that the seller is no longer bound to their previous agent and therefore is fair game.

In a few MLS's, you can also go after "Withdrawn" listings, but in most states and markets those sellers are still bound to an existing listing agreement, so you cannot prospect them. *Check with your broker before prospecting listings that are "Withdrawn."*

With new expired listings I always want to do everything possible to *contact them on the first day they show up as an expired*, and typically the earlier the better. I know that can feel like you're walking into a lion's den, but if you want to maximize your chances of getting the listing, *the first skilled agent to the punch has the best chance*. The longer you wait to call, the more annoyed they are likely to be, the less likely they are to even answer the phone, and the more likely they are to have already made a decision. So...

<u>Should I call them or knock on their door?</u> This question is a tradeoff between *efficiency* and *effectiveness*. Face to face conversations (i.e. at the door) will almost always get you better results. It also takes more time (and gas). Calling them by phone increases the number of sellers you can talk to in a day, but it's much easier for them to ignore you or hang up on you. Plus, it is more difficult to really connect with them, because you are just a voice on the other end of the phone rather than being a real person. Additionally, because more and more people no longer have home phones, it has become more difficult to reach people by phone.

The best strategy is a combination of calling and door-knocking. I have always used an expired subscription service that looks up owners' phone numbers, which I highly recommend you using because it allows you to use your time setting appointments rather than searching for phone numbers.

Call all the new expired and cancelled listings first thing every day. And then go door-knock the ones that are owner-occupied and in your core market area. Your core market area is the neighborhoods that are relatively close to your home and/or office and that are your preferred neighborhoods to do business. It can be very effective to actually drop by these hot prospects' homes in the morning on your way to your office. Catching them before they leave for work can be the best chance of connecting with them and setting a listing appointment.

FOR SALE BY OWNER (FSBO) SCRIPT

1. Hi, I'm calling about your house for sale by owner. Are you the owner? (Yes.) Great!
2. This is ______________ with ______________. The reason I'm calling is because...I work with a lot of buyers and sellers in your area…and wanted to find out …what I can do to help you? ( ) Great!
3. By the way, again my name is ____________…what is your name? ( ) Hi, ___________.
4. So _________, how much time will you take...before you might...decide to hire a strong agent...to...get your property sold...for you? ( ) Excellent!
5. When you...sell this house…where are you going next? ( ) That's exciting!
6. How soon do you need/want to be there? ( ) Great!
7. Why did you...decide to make the move? ( ) Terrific!/Ouch!
8. How would you rate your motivation to...sell your house right now...low, medium, or high? ( ) Good for you!
9. How are you marketing it? ( ) That's great!

10. How did you determine the price you're asking? ( ) Fantastic!

11. Do you have any flexibility on your price...or are you firm? ( ) Terrific!

12. Why did you decide to market the house yourself…rather than...hire a professional agent? ( ) That makes sense!

13. If you were to...hire an agent...what would you expect from them? ( ) Excellent!

14. Have you heard about the strategies I use to sell homes for top dollar? ( ) Really!

15. __________, if I could help you...get your property sold...and ______________ [*motivation*] ...and still net you the money you need in your pocket…would you...consider interviewing me now? ( ) Perfect!

16. When would be the best time for us to...get together...would tomorrow at 4:15 work...or would __________ at 2:15 be better? ( ) Excellent!

YesMaster Strategy: FSBO's are very likely to eventually hire an agent to sell their property. Call them as soon as they hit the market. The sooner you call them the better you will stay on their mental radar. Do not B.S. them by pretending you have a buyer. This script is a straightforward conversation about helping them get a result, and you will be amazed at how often you can set a legitimate listing appointment with them on your very first conversation when you use this script.

The key is to not be adversarial or stumped by a FSBO's responses. No matter what they say, treat them as totally normal responses and *do not be intimidated by anything they say*. Remember, they have worked on their "scripts" too, and their script is typically designed to deflect any conversation about listing the property or setting a listing appointment. *Simply repeat and affirm the FSBO's answers and then move on to the next question.* Never make them feel stupid or wrong.

If you are wondering how you can actually help FSBO's get a better result by hiring you, you may want to check out an advanced training program I have for listing FSBO's and Expireds called "FX Extreme."

FSBO PRE-APPOINTMENT OBJECTIONS/QUESTIONS:

OBJECTION: "Bring me a buyer." or "I'm willing to pay an agent who has a buyer...but I'm not going to list."

Excellent! So you are willing to… cooperate with an agent… that has a buyer. Great!

OBJECTION: "We're selling it ourselves"

So...right now you're just planning to do it yourself. Excellent!

OBJECTION: "We're not going to list."

So right now you're not really planning to...hire an agent. Got it!

> **YESMaster Strategy:** When they say they are going to do something or not do something that does not lead the conversation in the right direction, notice that you modify what you are reflecting (repeating) back to them. Instead of saying, "So you're not going to list," you reflect back simply that this is their plan for the moment: "So *right now* you're not *really planning to…________*." Notice, you have downgraded their statement from absolute certainty to simply their current intention.

> This is so powerful, because if they are genuinely motivated to sell, it is in their best interest to hire a professional agent. If you repeat that they are not going to list, you are literally affirming a course of action that it *not* the wisest course of action for them.

<u>OBJECTION:</u> "Do you have a buyer?"

That's a great question. We do have a number of buyers...however I'm not calling today because of a specific buyer for your property. What I do is find buyers for people... like yourself…who you want to… sell your home. So you are willing to...cooperate with an agent...that has a buyer, correct? (Yes.) Fantastic.

[AND THEN...Go back to the next question on the FSBO Script.]

<u>OBJECTION</u>: "We're not ready to list with an agent..."

1. So for now you're planning to just do it yourself. Got it.
2. And…I'm not saying you should...hire me right now. All I'm going to do is give you some valuable information to help you... get more money in your pocket. Obviously, you do want as much money in your pocket as possible...correct? (Yes.) Exactly!
3. When would be the best time for you to... get together with me... so we can go over that...Wednesday at 4:15 or would Thursday at 2:15 be better?"

<u>OBJECTION:</u> "We're still going to keep trying For-Sale-By-Owner for at least another month."

1. Excellent. And…I'm not trying to get you to...stop trying to sell it yourself. I'm simply interested in helping you get the result you want...which is to...get your home sold...in the best time possible, with the least amount of hassle, and net you the most money possible in your pocket, right? (Yes.)
2. Because that's what you want, isn't it? (Yes.) Excellent!
3. When would be the best time for you to...get together with me... so we can go over some options...Wednesday at 4:15 or would Thursday at 2:15 be better?"

OPEN HOUSE EVENT INVITE FOR DOOR-KNOCKING

Hi, my name is ________________ with ________________. I wanted to drop by and let you know about an Open House Event we are going to be holding for the ________ (Smiths) over on ____________ (address) this ____________ from _____ to _____ (E.g. Sunday from 1 to 4)*… [HAND THEM FLYER.]

I wanted to invite you to…come by… and…take a look….(mention any special treats or refreshments, etc) ….and also I wanted to find out…

1. Who do you know that would like to move into our area? ( ) Fantastic! Look forward to seeing you there!
2. Just out of curiosity…when do you think you might be ready to...make a move? ( ) Wow!
3. How long have you lived here? (10 yrs) Great!
4. Where did you move from? ( ) Good For You!
5. What brought you to this area? ( ) Excellent!
6. If you were to...move again… where do you think you would go next? ( ) That's Exciting!
7. And how soon would you like to do that? ( ) Terrific!!

If their time frame is 60 days or less...

8. It sounds like our next step would be to…set up a time to… get together… and take a look at the best way to make all this happen for you…so you can get to ______________ by ____________. Won't that be exciting? ( ) Fantastic!
9. Which would be the best time for us to get together…Monday at 4:15...or Tuesday at 4:15 pm?

If their time frame is longer than 3 months...add them to your Personal Circle®

> **YESMaster Strategy:** *Here is a great way to connect with other homeowners in the neighborhood and to position you as their *"go-to agent."* Set up the first hour of the event to be a "Neighbors-Only Open House Preview." You can even encourage the homeowners to be home for this first part if they want. This gives you the opportunity to have a more casual opportunity to connect with future sellers by creating basically a simple "mini-block party," and *you* are the host!
>
> The script that you add to the beginning is: "And…before the public open house, we're going to be hosting a *Special NEIGHBORS ONLY PREVIEW* from Noon to 1:00. We'll have refreshments and the __________ (owners) will be there, and you can…check out their home…and say "Hi." It's going to be awesome! ( )

OPEN HOUSE EVENT INVITE VS JUST-LISTED SCRIPT

Agents often ask why I do not use the traditional "Just-Listed" script. There is nothing technically wrong with using a "Just-Listed" script. However, there are a couple of inherent disadvantages with that approach.

First, the "Just-Listed" script is framed to primarily find buyers rather than sellers. *The power of verbal frames is significant.* Stated simply, you get what you ask for…and if you are asking if someone knows a potential buyer (e.g. "Who do you know that would like to move into the neighborhood?") the script is verbally framed to find buyers. I want you to primarily focus on finding sellers.

Second, it simply feels too much like you are soliciting. You are looking for something from the person standing at the door. You are there to "get" something. People automatically put up resistance any time they feel they are being solicited

The "Open House Event Invite" is an "*invitation*," not a solicitation. You are essentially inviting them to a party. People love invitations. And neighboring homeowners love to see what their neighbor's house really looks like on the inside (especially when it is staged). Once the invitation is delivered, the person's resistance to you is lowered, then you ask the personal question, "When do you think you might be ready to…make a move?" almost as an after-thought.

For more on using the "Open House Event Invite" effectively (including "the Columbo Technique"), go to www.thebookofyes.com/bonuses.

HOT MARKET SCRIPT

Hi, my name is ____________________ with _________________! I was dropping by (calling) to give you a quick update on the real estate market in _______. ...And to let you know there have been ____ homes that have sold in the last ______ days … and that ____ of those sold in less than 30 days (OR …sold at or above list price!)! Did you know that? ( ) Yeah, it's pretty exciting news, isn't it?

And we know that when homes start selling like that …more will sell very quickly … So I was just wondering ….

1. When do you think you might be ready to...make a move? (Never/Not sure.) Great!
2. How long have you lived here? (5 years) Good for you!
3. Where did you move from? ( ) Excellent!
4. What brought you to this area? ( ) Wonderful!
5. If you were to...move again… where do you think you go next? ( ) That's Exciting!
6. And how soon would you like to do that? ( ) Terrific!!

<u>If their time frame is 30 days or less...</u>

7. It sounds like our next step would be to…set up a time to get together…and take a look at the best way to make all this happen for you…so you can get to ______________ by ____________. Won't that be exciting? (Yes.) Fantastic!

8. Which would be the best time for us to get together…Monday at 4:15...or Tuesday at 4:15 pm?

<u>If their time frame is longer than 30 days...</u>*add them to your Personal Circle® (PC) and call them at least monthly so when they are ready to move, you are on their mental "radar." If you feel they may be ready in less than a month, treat them as a lead and touch base with them every week.*

> **YESMaster Strategy:** Make sure you get their contact information. Use the **PERSONAL CIRCLE MULTIPLIER SCRIPT** below to get their information.

HOT MARKET SCRIPT VS. JUST-SOLD SCRIPT

When you knock on someone's door to tell them about your accomplishment, "I just sold a house!" they are not nearly as excited about your personal victory as you are.

The "Just-Sold" script sounds agent-centric. In other words, it's about YOU. "Look what I just did." "I just sold a listing…" The immediate internal response from the other person is, "So what? Why do I care what you just did?" That thought immediately causes resistance.

The Hot Market script makes the conversation about the market, not about you. People who own homes in a neighborhood are interested in things happening in the real estate market that impacts the value of their property. They have a vested interest in that. They do not have a vested interest in hearing about something you just did.

Second, it easily comes across as soliciting. "Why would you knock on my door to tell me about the house you just sold unless you're trying to convince me to sell?"

The Hot Market approach offers exciting information of value to the homeowner about what the real estate market is doing. You are giving them a quick "market update." That automatically makes it about them because it directly affects the value of their home, whether they are interested in selling or not.

PERSONAL CIRCLE MULTIPLIER SCRIPT

YesMaster Strategy: If they have no plans to move now or in near future, your goal is to connect and exchange contact information with them. This script is to help you accomplish that goal.

Well, ___________...it's a pleasure to meet you today... Who do you know in the area who **is** looking to...buy or sell or invest in real estate... in the near future that I could help?

When you do run across someone who needs to sell or buy real estate...do you have a great "go-to" agent to refer them to? (No/Not Really.*) Perfect! Let me be your go-to agent...ok? (Sure.)

*If they say they already have an agent: "Good for you! I'd love to be your back up."

Why don't we... exchange information and... stay in touch? Do you have a business card? [*If not, let them put their information on the back of your business card.*]

Let me shoot you a quick email or text so you can...keep my information in your phone...and when you... need me... you'll have it. What's your cell number? (____) Great. And what's your email address?

[*If they show any reluctance...*] And (chuckle) don't worry...you're not going to get spammed or anything like that...'cause I hate that as much as you do. Know what I mean? (Yes.) Great.

So [*with a smile*] what's the number/email you...want me...to use?

OR

I provide my personal clients a detailed market update every month and free personal Market Analysis any time they want it. I assume you do like to know about trends in real estate that are affecting the value of your home, right? (Yes.) Great! What email address would you...like me... to use?

OR [*if they will not give you their contact information*]

If you would like to check it out...here's my card. Just... go to my website at [myagentsite].com/marketupdate and you can...request it...if you...decide you want it. Sound great? (Yes.) Excellent!

The "Market Update" webpage on your site is a simple opt-in page where they can sign up for your monthly email market updates.

YESMaster Strategy: You always get what you expect! Be confident and comfortable when you ask for their information and they will give it to you almost every time.

Use your iPad with the app, "Open Home Pro" as another way to get their information by carrying it with you. For some reason people often feel more comfortable putting their information into an iPad.

LEAD FOLLOW UP SCRIPT

1. Hi, ________. This is ________________ with ________________. We spoke last week and you were thinking you were going to... be ready to ___________________... in the next _________________. I wanted to touch base and see....are you still on track with that time frame? (Yes.) Excellent.
2. And....you <u>do</u> still...want to buy/sell....at that time, correct? (Yes.) Perfect.
3. I was wondering...what questions do you have...or....information do you need....that I can get for you? ( ) Fantastic!
4. So...it sounds like we should set up a time to...get together _________ [e.g. "next week"]....to go over that... Which would be better for you....Wednesday at 2:15 or would Thursday be better?

YESMaster Strategy: When talking to a lead, use the phrase "touch base" instead of "follow up." Following up is a *resistance trigger* for most people, because no one likes to be followed (except on Twitter).

Only set an appointment if they are motivated to do something now. If not, keep them in your lead folder if you need to follow up with them again in less than a month. If they are over 30 days out from being ready to start the selling or buying process, put them in your Personal Circle "A-Team" and call them monthly to stay on their mental radar.

POWERFUL QUESTIONS FOR LEAD FOLLOW-UP

These questions can be used in many situations to identify and clarify motivation.

- So… if you could ______________________________ [fill in their motivation]...Is that something….
    a. ….that you would still...be excited...about?
    b. ….that you are still interested in/committed to doing?
    c. ….that would still be good for you financially?
- How would you rate your motivation to….._______________________...on a scale of 1 to 10?
- Tell me more about that….
- So…what's important to you about that?
- *Reverse Motivation*: "It sounds to me like you should stay where you are….why are you wanting to buy/sell right now?"

> **YESMaster Strategy**: The "Reverse Motivation" is an excellent question to use when they have indicated a desire to sell, and then they begin back-peddling or giving reasons why they do not want to put their house on the market or they start acting like they're not motivated to sell. Do not be afraid to "call their bluff."

SELLER SHEET: Pre-Qualifying Script

Source: ____________ Contact Date: ____________

Listing Appt. Date: ______________ Time: ______________

Name: ____

Address: ____

Phone: ____________________________

Email: ____________________________

1. Before I come out…I need to get a little more information from you…so I can do my homework. Do you have a couple of minutes? Great!
2. When we get together, if everything looks good,* and you…feel confident…I am the best agent to…sell your property...are you planning to…hire me…when we meet? ___ Terrific!
3. Are you interviewing any other agents…or am I the only one?** _______________ Good!
4. When you...sell this property…where are you moving?___________________. Fantastic!
5. What's taking you to ________? (OR) Why are you making the move? ___________________. Good for you!
6. How soon do you want to be there? ________________________________. Great!

7. If we…sell your home in less than 30 days…would that be a problem for you? ______ Excellent!
8. What would happen if your property just didn't sell? ________________________. Really!
9. What price are you thinking you would like to… list your property for… realistically?___________.
10. And of course, I research the market every day...so obviously, we'll make sure we…list your home… at a price that will…get it sold, correct? _________ Perfect!
11. What do you think is the lowest price you would consider? ___________________ Got it.
12. How much do you owe on the property? _________________. Good!
13. Have you thought about trying it for-sale-by-owner? (No/Yes) Terrific/Got it!
14. Will you briefly tell me about your home?

    ____

Bed: _________	Baths: _______	Garage: _______
Pool: _____ Lot: ___________________________		
Special Features:		

15. How would you rate the condition of your home...from 1 to 10…10 being like brand new?__
16. What would it take to make it like new? ____
17. Besides that...is there anything else positive or negative that buyers might notice_________
18. I'm going to send you some information for our meeting, will you go through it before we meet? ______

19. What questions do you have, if any, before you're ready to...get the ball rolling... and...put me to work for you? ______________
____

20. And last thing, will _______ [all decision-makers]*...be there...for our appointment?** (Yes) Perfect!

21. I look forward to seeing you __________ at __________!

PRE-QUALIFYING NOTES:

2.*For FSBO's add: "and the numbers work..."

3.**[IF "YES," they are interviewing other agents] "Can I safely assume you won't…make a decision…until after you…meet with me, correct?" (Yes.) Excellent!

18.*<u>Normal Contents of the Pre-Listing Pack</u>: Your Action Plan/Brochure, CMA, Net Sheet, Listing agreement and disclosure documents. Optional: Personalized video, Testimonials/Reviews, and/or any web links, samples, etc.

20. *If you know, for example that it is a married couple, say, "And last thing, will both you and your husband/wife…be there…for our appointment?" The key is to clarify that all decision-makers will be there. If you do not know, ask: "Besides you, who are the other decision-makers…or others you'll want to talk to before deciding?"

20. [***IF they answer "**NO**" to this question regarding **all decision-makers present***] Then let's do this...let's find a time when all of us can meet...that way we can make sure both/all of your questions are answered and that you and __________...feel comfortable… hiring me to… sell your home. Because obviously I will be working for both of you, right? (Yes.) ...And I want both of you to… know you're making the right decision… yes? (Yes.) Perfect.

> **YESMaster Strategy:** <u>DO NOT</u> handle objections during the pre-qualifying phase. Remember the *only goal* before you meet is getting the appointment and making sure they are motivated to sell.

THE LISTING PRESENTATION SCRIPTS

THE LISTING PRESENTATION

1. Hi __________. Thanks for having me over! Are you excited about moving to __________? Would it be OK if I gave myself a quick tour?
2. If it's OK...let's use the kitchen table, so we can lay everything out.
3. [*As sitting down*] Let's talk about getting you to ______________ [*motivation*]!

CONFIRMING MOTIVATION

4. Now, the first thing I'd like to do is…review your situation and…what's important to you about making this move…is that OK? [Review & confirm SELLER SHEET Questions 4-13] Fantastic!
5. Now...I have three bottom line questions for you. Are you ready?

   #1 Are you definitely ready to… sell your property? (Yes.) Fantastic!

   #2 Will you…price it where it will sell… or are you OK just keeping it on the market for a long time? (Yes/Not Sure) Great!

   #3. And most important, _________...Do you… want me… to… get it sold… for you? ( ) Terrific!

[If they say "yes," go to ***PRICING****. If not, go to* ***CONFIRMING THE GOAL****.]*

CONFIRMING THE GOAL

6. _______________, the purpose of our meeting today is two-fold:
   #1. Is for me to provide you with some very important information about what it's going to take to…get your house sold… for top dollar… so you can… get to _________ by _________ [*motivation*] …right? (Yes.)
   #2. Is for us to… decide today... if the right thing for you is to...partner with me …in the sale of your home. Does that sound fair enough? (Yes.) Excellent!
7. And whether you…decide to hire me…or not….I hope it will become clear to you through our meeting….that my goal is to help you get what ***you*** want. If I can't help you...I'll tell you today…because I'm not interested in just getting a listing. I'm **very** interested in helping you get to _______________ [*motivation*]. …Because that's what you want, right? (Yes.) Then we're on the same page!**
8. Now… There is really one key item for us to address today…and that is to…determine the right price… to set on your home… that will cause it to sell, right? Because obviously you don't want to… put it on the market… to have it **not** sell, correct?
9. Here's what I will do… as soon as you… decide to hire me... I am going to do everything it takes through my Action Plan to…get your home exposed… to all of the qualified buyers in the market…because that is the kind of exposure you want, right? (Yes.) Great!
10. So the key today is for us to… establish the right price… that will make those qualified Buyers excited about your house when they see it. Does that make sense?

CMA PRESENTATION:

11. In preparing for our meeting, I did a thorough Market Study for your home...also called a Comparative Market Analysis…Are you familiar with this? (Yes/No) Perfect!
12. There are 3 main parts to the market study: (*point to each section as you explain it*)
    A. First are <u>Active Listings</u>. These are your competition, right? I call this "*<u>Dream Land</u>*"…because…it's what people <u>want</u> to get for their house...but you don't know...what it's actually going to sell for…right?
    B. Second are <u>Expired Listings</u>. Do you know what these are? ( ) That's right, homes that didn't sell at all. They wanted to sell, but something went wrong. I call this "*<u>Never Never Land</u>*." Can you see why? ( ) Exactly. …Because you NEVER want to be here, right?
    C. Last are the <u>SOLD</u> houses. This is "*<u>REALITY</u>*." Because it tells us what homes are actually going for in this market. Are you with me? (Yes.) Excellent.
13. So this [Point to SOLDs.] is where we'll focus today…because obviously...to get you to __________ by __________ [motivation], in which of these three categories do we...want your house to end up? (SOLD.) Exactly!
14. The *purpose* of the Market Analysis…is to determine the *value* of your home…
    A. First, as Buyers will look at it... and second as an appraiser will look at it... I'm sure you can understand why that's important, right?
    B. First...the appraiser, because that's who the lender will hire to determine the value of your house based on what comparable homes are actually selling for...which

is what Buyers are actually paying ***now***. Does that make sense?

C. Second, to make sure we price your home in a way that will…make it attractive to Buyers. Because…Is a BUYER only going to look at your home…or… are they going to shop around and compare your home with others? (Compare.) Obviously!

D. So as they look at houses…what do you think they are comparing? ( ) Exactly. They are comparing the features, such as quality, condition, and location, AND...they are comparing price, right?

15. Are you ready to take a look? [*GO THROUGH the CMA with them, start with ACTIVE. Focus on SOLDS.*]

    A. This home is comparable to yours…

    B. Notice, how many bedrooms? ( ) How many baths? ( ) How big is the garage? ( ) What year was it built? ( ) How many square feet? ( ) [*Wait for them to answer, and then affirm each answer.*]

    C. Have you seen this home? *[Explain...comparing features of each property...]*

        1. Your house has more value than this one...because…[explain why]
        2. [OR] This property is a little nicer than yours...because…[explain why]
        3. [OR] This property is very comparable to yours…[*explain why*]
        4. Does that make sense?

    D. What was/is their price?

    E. Notice how long on the market?* How's that going to work to get you to ________ by ________ [motivation]?

16. So based on what the market is telling us… what price do you feel will… get Buyers excited… about choosing your property over our competition?

PRICING

17. After looking at your house and reviewing what the market is telling us... I'm suggesting we… list the house for $_______________. ...And you can see why that's the right price, correct?
18. Because…that will get you the *best* price for your home in this market, in the *best* time possible…so we can get you to __________ by __________ [their motivation]. Won't that be exciting!? ( ) Fantastic.
19. Do you have any questions about anything we've covered? ( ). Are you ready for the next step?

NET SHEET PRESENTATION

20. The net sheet gives you all the costs associated with selling your house...and how much you are actually going to walk away with after the sale of your house. That is something you would like to know, correct?
    A. [GO THROUGH NET SHEET WITH THEM]
21. These are all standard closing fees and expenses for Sellers. Any questions on that?
    A. [FINISH SHOWING OR CALCULATING THEIR NET]
22. Based on a realistic sales price of $___________ and a closing date of_________…here are the ESTIMATED total net proceeds to you at closing (and after your tax escrow refund)... [CIRCLE THE NET $ AMOUNT]
23. ____________, is that a number you can live with? (Yes/No.)

A. *[If they say yes, go to DECISION. If not:]* I understand…it's less than you were expecting. Is it a number you could live with if you had to? (Yes.) Excellent.

DECISION

24. So we'll...get it on the market at $__________… which we agreed is the right price, correct? (Yes.) Excellent!
25. Well… I'm ready for you to… put me to work! Are you ready… for the next step? (Yes.) Awesome!
26. Can I lay out for you what's going to happen next? Here are the highlights...
    A. First, we want to...make sure the house shows at its best, right?...[explain staging, etc.]
    B. Second, I will be preparing the marketing for your property and...launch my pre-marketing campaign immediately...because you did...want us...to get the most exposure to the market as fast as possible, correct? (Yes.) Perfect.
    C. Next, we launch...our **Exclusive 10-Day Marketing Blitz**!®* Sound exciting?
    D. Your property will be marketed to every potential buyer out there, and promoted to every licensed Realtor and their buyers through the Multiple Listing Service. Plus...I have it syndicated to over 5,200 real estate websites...including all the most popular ones buyers go to online. Of course, you understand how important that kind of internet exposure is for you, right? (Yes.) Excellent.
    E. [*Go through the other highlights of your plan...*] Because you do...want me to give you the right exposure… that

will get the best buyers in here, right? (Yes.) Awesome. Because that's exactly what you're going to get with me.

F. And with that exposure, assuming the market responds as we expect, we will be getting lots of buyer traffic. I'll be following up with all of that...which will then give us the best offers. Then I'll be negotiating all offers we get...to ultimately... get your property sold... for top dollar... and get you ______________ [motivation]. Are you ready for that? (Yes!) Great!

G. So...are you ready to...start packing? ( ) ...I don't mean today...but soon! (Yes.) Perfect.

27. Any questions...before you're ready to...** let me help you... make this move happen... and get to __________ [motivation]? (We're ready.) Awesome!
28. I'm going to have you... initial right here... on the CMA and the Net Sheet***...And then we'll take care of the rest of the paperwork... and I'll get to work! Congratulations! *[Shake their hand and proceed to signatures.]*

---

*[OR whatever action plan you use.]

**[OR] "...or are you ready to..."

***[*Put your initials first and a spot for theirs and let them initial.]*

LISTING PRESENTATION PRICING OBJECTIONS:

"That's not enough." Or "That's too low." Or "We have to get more than that."

I understand… that's less than you were hoping for. [Pause] However, you can see why that's the right price, right? ...Based on what the market is actually telling us. (yes.) Excellent.

"Can we start higher?" Or "We want to try it at a higher price."

1. Of course…that's always an option…to test the market, right?
2. You want the good news or bad news first? (Good/Bad.) The good news is...these sellers (point to comparables that have been on the market a long time) have already done that for us. Does that make sense? [Explain how many price reductions they have had, etc.]
3. So the reality is... starting at a high price actually works against you. That's the bad news, right? ( ) Exactly
4. Because the best time to get top-dollar in this market is when a home first hits the market. You do want top dollar, right? (Of course!) Absolutely!
5. That's why…as you can see…$_________ is the right price…to get the most buyer interest fast…which will always get you the best price. Make sense?

[OPTIONAL:]

And this is why it's important to... understand the Buyer's perspective. ...Because what they see *before* they see the house...is the *price*...and because it's higher than the competition... the price actually makes them *afraid* to fall in love with your house. So... they actually come to see your house...trying *NOT* to fall in love with it...just because of the *price*. [PAUSE]

And your house may be perfect for them, but they feel the price forces them to say "no."

Are you beginning to see why I'm concerned about pricing it high?

The Story Comparable Properties Tell

Always be prepared to explain the number of price reductions a listing has had along with days on the market, because it tells a story that can help keep the seller from making the same mistake. Also be prepared to show how homes were positioned in the market that sold fast or for full price or above. *The more you know about the statistics, the more powerful you will be.*

A Sold listing may show 146 total days on market. The obvious conclusion would be that it took 146 to get it sold. However, when you look at the listing history on the MLS (multiple listing service), it may tell a different story. What if, for example, the listing had three price reductions, one after thirty days, another after 96 days, and a 3rd reduction after 140 days? That tells a totally different story which can be very powerful when shared with the seller. It didn't actually take 146 days to sell. *They spent 140 days testing the market, and then once they got to the right price, it only took 6 days to get it sold!*

Your job is to be *the expert* and to have the certainty to help them avoid making the same mistake. It costs them time and money, and makes your job more difficult.

LISTING PRESENTATION GUIDE NOTES:

#2) Your initial walk through the home should be brief. Take notes of key items you notice and that's all. You can do a thorough walk-through after they hire you. If they insist on giving you a tour, focus mostly on asking them questions about their motivation for moving.

#3,#6,#7,etc.) _________[motivation] - Every time you see a blank with "[motivation],' you are going to fill in the blank with whatever their primary motivation is...such as:

- "...San Diego by the end of summer!"
- "...your new home on the golf course!"
- "...your new job in Phoenix!"
- "...out from under all this financial stress."

Remember, their motivation is your leverage to help them make the decision to hire you.

#4) The **SELLER SHEET** has all the pre-qualifying questions you ask before going on the appointment to clarify their motivation and to identify potential objections so you can be prepared.

#5-3) If they say "yes" to hiring you up front, skip to *pricing* only if:

- They know and trust you enough to price it where you recommend.
- You feel confident that they are actually ready to sign the listing agreement at the right price. (if you skip to PRICING and then run into resistance, go back immediately to CONFIRMING THE GOAL.)

#5-3) If you know you are competing with other agents add: "What would you want to see today, so that you can...feel absolutely confident...in making your decision to...partner with me...in the sale of your property?"

#12) At this point, show them the CMA, but do NOT hand it to them. Keep it in your hand as you explain the 3 parts to them. (If you hand it to them, they will immediately stop listening to you and start reading it and interpreting it on their own.) And as you explain each part, use your other hand to firmly point to each section "Dream Land," "Never,Never Land," and "Reality" as you describe them.

The key to getting sellers to accept a realistic price for their property, is helping them to associate pain with the prices of Active (Dream Land) and Expired listings (Never Never Land) and to associate pleasure (Reality) with Sold listings. Nobody wants to think of themselves as living in "Dream Land" or "Never Never Land." This process is called "Visual Anchoring" in NLP, and is very powerful in getting them to list at the right price.

#13) "So this…" You want to be pointing to the SOLDS section of the CMA as you say this. This is part of the visual anchoring process.

#15) As you ask them each question, "How many bedrooms?" etc., it is critical that you *let them give the answer*. I know it sounds weird, but when they read the data on the CMA out loud, they are subconsciously confirming that they accept the data as true. Once they do this, they are much less likely to argue with you or with the CMA about the validity of the information as it relates to setting a realistic price on their home.

Start with ACTIVE listings and then move to SOLD listings. You want to go over each of the relevant comparables by asking them the questions and letting them answer. As they answer, affirm the answer by repeating it. Once they get into it, they will often literally start reading the Market Analysis to you. This is perfect, because it means they are acknowledging the information is true.

What makes this Listing Presentation so powerful and effective?

1. Because it is question-based. Asking effective questions keeps the Sellers engaged and allows them to lead themselves to a decision to hire you, rather than you simply telling them stuff. Questions also help you maintain control of the direction of the meeting. After every question it is very important that you: 1) wait for them to answer and 2) repeat and affirm their response every time it's appropriate.
2. Because the listing presentation focuses on the Seller and on what the Seller wants (i.e. motivation), rather than on what you are going to do. After all, it's about them, not about you. Most listing presentations are agent-centered which is mostly useful for putting the sellers to sleep.
3. Because it repeatedly affirms that your primary interest is helping them get the results they want, not what you want. "CONFIRMING THE GOAL" is designed to clearly put you on their side. Once they believe and feel that you are genuinely there for them, most of their resistance disappears.
4. Because the CMA Presentation uses visual and psychological anchors ("Dream Land," "Never-Never Land," and "Reality") to educate and lead the Seller to correctly interpret the Market Analysis to arrive at the right list price that will cause the home to sell. The effect is that the Seller subconsciously rejects the pricing of Active Listings and will avoid pricing their home in a way that would cause the listing to expire, thereby sending them to "Never-Never Land." After all, how much time does a motivated seller want to spend in Dreamland or Never-Never Land? None. So when skillfully presented, it is very

powerful at leading the Seller to agree to an accurate price from the beginning.

5. Because it shifts the Seller's thinking regarding the value of their property to see it from the Buyers' perspective and the Appraiser's perspective rather than from their own biased point of view.
6. Because it forces the Seller to read the Market Analysis to you, rather than you reading it to him/her. This is a critical step on #15 of the presentation. As long as you are the one reading the CMA to them, they can subconsciously reject the validity of the comparable sales, but the moment they start reading the details of each house to you, they psychologically are acknowledging the truth of the numbers. This is one of the points where it is critical to develop the skill and confidence to get them to read it to you.
7. Because it bases the pricing of their home squarely on what the market is dictating by comparable sales. And the PRICING section makes sure there is agreement on price before proceeding with the presentation. <u>If you leave the CMA before you get their agreement on price, you will get killed on the pricing objections.</u>
8. Because it covers the closing costs in a way that makes them a normal part of the process and addresses how much they will net in their pocket at closing.
9. Because DECISION leads them through a process of imagining their *home-selling journey* with you as their agent ending with the successful top-dollar sale of their home and them packing, rather than by focusing on listing and marketing process. Sellers do not care about the marketing or the process, they only care about the result. The bottom line effect of this visualization process (#25-27) is that when you get to a decision question at the end, they are not

thinking about hiring you, they are thinking about the end result of what happens after they hire you!

10. Because this presentation never asks the Sellers a "Yes"-or-"No"-decision question. Instead it gives them two optional answers that are both positive (#27). They can answer, "We're ready" or "We have more questions." *Either answer leads you and them forward, not backward.* A traditional closing question, such as, "Will you list your home with me today?" puts the seller in a position of telling you "no." And once they tell you "no" it is much more difficult for them to retract their "no" and give you a "yes."
11. Because it lets them formalize the decision first by simply initialing non-binding information, followed by a celebratory response ("Congratulations!") and a handshake. Emotionally they have already agreed to hire you at this point. The natural next step is to take care of the paperwork which concludes with the binding signatures.
12. Because it removes the *Resistance Triggers* used in most listing presentation scripts. Resistance Triggers are words and phrases that automatically cause people to resist you and what you're saying. Most of the time they are not even aware of why they are resisting. It usually ends up with them telling you they are not ready to make a decision or they need to "think about it."

To learn more about Resistance Triggers you may be accidentally using, go to www.thebookofyes.com/bonuses

GUARANTEED SALE SCRIPT:

***[If you are offering a Guaranteed Sale, insert this conversation normally between #7 and #8 in the Listing Presentation]*

You were also interested in the GUARANTEED SALE, correct? (Yes.)

The way this works is very simple... [go over highlights of your terms sheet]

1. First, we make sure we price your home accurately and strategically to generate maximum Buyer interest...which will always get us the best price. Make sense?
2. Second, we make sure your home is in "showcase" condition when buyers come through so they are ...sold ...on your home. So we will schedule our professional stager to come in and go over with you how to ...get your home looking at its best for Buyers. Because we do...want Buyers to fall in love with your house, right? (YES.) Absolutely.
3. And then, I'll be getting to work to… get your property sold… in the next _____ days for top dollar! Sound great? (YES.) Excellent.
4. Do you have any questions about how the guarantee works? (No.) Good.

[Continue with Listing Presentation #8]

If you want to learn more about how to create and offer an effective, no-B.S. Guaranteed Sale, check out www.DoubleYourListingPower.com

BUYER SCRIPTS

BUYER SHEET: Pre-Qualifying Script

Source: ________________ Contact Date: ____________________

Appt. Date: __________________ Time: ____________________

Name: ____

Address: ____

Phone: ________________ **Email:** _________________________

Referral from ____

Property Address: _______________________________________

1. How soon would you like to be in your home? __________
2. How long have you been seriously looking? ____________
3. Have you seen any homes/areas you really like? ________
4. [OPTIONAL] What's important to you about buying a house right now? ______________
5. Do you already have a good Buyer's Agent working with you? __________________
6. How much money do you have set aside for down payment and closing costs? ____________
7. Have you already started working with a mortgage company/lender? ____________
    a.) (If YES) Great! Do you have your pre-approval letter from them? _______ Great!

b.) (If NO) Great! I have some great lenders I work with…I will have one of them give you a call and… get you pre-approved. It's no cost or obligation for you…but it will give us extra leverage in getting the best price on the home you choose…because it lets the seller and their agent know that you are qualified.

8. Do you have a home to sell before you close on your next home? ______________
9. Are you currently in a lease? ________ When is your lease up? ______________
10. Besides you, are there any other decision makers? __________________________
11. Tell me briefly what you're looking for…
12. Price Range: _______________ Areas: ________________
    Bedrooms: ________ Baths: ________ Garage: ________
    Pool: _________ Lot: _____

Special needs/considerations:

13. Fortunately, it sounds like our next step to get you one step closer to your new home, is to…set up a time… to… get together…so we can get on the computer and …start finding you the house you want…won't that be great?!
14. So which is better for you…__________ or __________?

BUYER CALL ASKING FOR INFORMATION

Buyer: Hello. I was calling about the house for sale on Elm Street...what's the price they're asking?

AGENT: Absolutely, that is a great house! It's listed at $585,000….is that in the price range you're looking for?

Buyer: Well….possibly….do you have any homes in the area under $500,000?

AGENT: Absolutely! How soon are you looking to be in a new home? (this summer.) Fantastic!

AGENT: And buy the way….my name is _____________. What is your name? ( ) Hi, _____________.

[Go to Buyer Sheet #2…and continue the conversation]

KEY POINTS TO REMEMBER:

1. Ask questions. *Asking the right questions* (from the Buyer Sheet) *leads the conversation in the right direction.*

2. *No B.S.!* Do not use the amateur B.S. technique that some scripts teach of pretending like you have to look up the price, in order to keep them on the phone. Answer their question with enthusiasm and then immediately follow the answer with a straightforward question that keeps them engaged: "Is that in

the price range you're looking for?" Now you have started a conversation of exchanging information, rather than withholding information in order to keep them from hanging up. Go pro and master the skill of engaging people in a mutually beneficial conversation.

3. Be excited about what *they* are excited about, which is probably looking at houses and finding the perfect house. They are ***not*** excited about financing, so do not start pressuring them to meet with your lender up front. Set up a time to start the process of finding the perfect house for them, and then make talking to your lender secondary in the conversation. [E.g. "Awesome! So we'll get together tomorrow at 2:00 PM to start looking at houses. *In the meantime*, I'll have my lender give you quick call to get your loan pre-approval process started.]

4. Be interested! Be eager! Be curious! Be conversational....this is not an interrogation!

5. Ask for the appointment.

OPEN HOUSE EVENT SCRIPT

ICEBREAKER QUESTIONS:

1. Hi! Come on in! My name is ________________. Feel free to look around and...let me know if you have any questions…OK?
2. Have you been out looking at a lot of open houses this weekend…or is this your first one? ( ) Excellent!
3. Are you just out looking around…or are you actively in the market for a new home?

GOING DEEPER QUESTIONS: [Use as the conversation dictates.]

4. Do you own a home in the area? (Yes) Great! [Go to Open House Invite Script #2]
5. How well does this house match what you're looking for? ( ) Terrific!
6. Is this in the price range you're looking for…or are you looking for something different? ( ) Excellent!
7. How soon do you want to...be in a new home? ( ) Fantastic!
8. Do you…have a fantastic Buyers Agent representing you yet…or are you still on your own? (Not yet.) Excellent!
9. I would be happy to help you out. Do you have a list of the other open houses going on in the area today...or are you just cruising around? (Offer to email them a list of today's open houses.)

IF ACTIVELY LOOKING:

10. What's your next step?
11. I would be delighted to work with you and help you…get into a new home. When would be the best time for us to …get together …and start really finding the right home for you…are weekends best for you…or are you available during the week? ( ) Great!

GETTING OPEN HOUSE EVENT GUESTS TO REGISTER:

"Before you leave would you please...register...so the Seller can know how many people came by… Thanks!"

OR

"For Security purposes, the Seller is asking that all guests…register…before they go through the house. Thanks!"

YESMaster Strategy: One of the most effective strategies is to use an iPad (or comparable) using the Open Home Pro app (or comparable). There is no perfect time to ask guests to register. It is preferable that their first moment in the house allows them to feel the house, not pressure from an agent. Another effective strategy is to have a visible sign "Please Register" posted next to your iPad (but not next to the front door).

PRE-APPOINTMENT SELLER OBJECTIONS

BASIC RESPONSES TO OBJECTIONS OVER THE PHONE:

That's a great question...and obviously that's one of the things we'll go over when we meet. Fair enough?

OR

That's exactly why we should... get together... so we can go over that... Which works better for you...tomorrow at 2:15? ...Or would 4:15 be better?

YESMaster Strategy: Remember your only goal with a motivated seller at this point is to set an appointment. When you are prospecting, objections are used by sellers to avoid having to meet with you. They are trying to get just enough information to decide a meeting with you is *not* necessary. When you start trying to handle their objections or answer all their questions over the phone, they are looking for any reason to dismiss you.

Only answer objections that you *must* answer in order to get the appointment. All other objections you can answer during your listing presentation. That is what the above answers will accomplish for you. You are not dodging or avoiding their questions, you are simply deferring them until you are able to meet with them face to face. This puts you in a position to be able to lead them to a decision to hire you.

THE "DON'T HANG UP ON ME SCRIPT"

What do you say when someone is about to hang up on you? Well, in the first place it can be hard to tell when someone is going to actually hang up on you or not. Sometimes you will actually use this script after they hang up and you call them right back. I know…it sounds crazy…but it works! Try it.

[*Say very quickly.*] Wait, wait, wait, wait, wait!…don't hang up! Don't hang up!

Look…I know you're probably ________ (frustrated/sick of calls like this)…so let me just ask you this… [*And then proceed with the script.*]

YESMaster Strategy: Notice, "wait" is repeated 4 or 5 times with no pause. You want to say it very rapidly, almost staccato with a slight hint of desperation that creates a sense of urgency and importance to your message.

> The funny thing is that most of the time they will not hang up! There is something about our wiring as human beings that makes people say to themselves, "Anybody that wants to speak to me that badly, deserves at least a chance." They may still be just as mad or annoyed, but now you have their attention. It will probably feel uncomfortable the first few times you do this, but then you just go right on with the Expired Script (or whichever script is appropriate).

This script is all about learning how to break through ***resistance***. The beauty of this is that this prospect has figured out that hanging up makes most agents simply give up and go away without any argument, so hanging up is their "script."

When you call them back immediately after they hang up, all the competition has already been eliminated and so has this person's script. Often you will find that these are the nicest people, and that is why they hang up, because they know that if they stay on the line they are too nice to say "no." Be the agent who is willing to break through their resistance and you will be amazed how many appointments you get!

For another killer training video on "Breaking through Resistance with Tough Expireds" go to www.thebookofyes.com/bonuses.

"WE'RE TAKING THE HOUSE OFF THE MARKET." OR "WE'RE TAKING A BREAK." OR "WE DECIDED NOT TO SELL."

I see. ...So if you had sold this house, where were you planning to go next? ( ) Awesome!

So what's taking you to ___________ (e.g. L.A.)? ( ) Excellent!

So it sounds like you're definitely going to be moving to ___________ (L.A.) at some point in the future, correct? (*Yes.*) And you will be...selling your home, correct? (*Yes.*) It's just a matter of whether to... do it now... or at some point in the future...right?

If you could... do it sooner rather than later... is that something you would... be excited... about? *(I guess./Sure./We're just tired of trying.)* Got it.

Let's do this...let's...set up a time to get together and just... take a look at the options... and see what it would take to actually ___________ (get your home sold and get you to ___________ by _________). Wouldn't that be great? (*Yes.*)

Great! So which would be better for you...Monday at 4:15 or would 5:15 be better?

YESMaster Strategy: Remember to repeat and affirm their answer. You always want to acknowledge their perspective. See their question as an opportunity to build a connection, not as a threat to be attacked.

"WE'RE GOING TO RE-LIST WITH THE SAME AGENT"

Have you already signed a new listing agreement? (*No.*) Great!

So…what I would be wondering is this…. What new strategies is the agent going to use in the next ____ months, …that they didn't already try… in the last _____ months…when they had it on the market before? Does that make sense? ( )

….Because obviously… you don't want to… put the house back on the market… to have it NOT sale again, right? (*Right.*) Exactly.

If you could… sell your home… in the next 30 days, would that pose a problem for you? (No.) Excellent!

All we will need is about 15 minutes together for me to share with you some things that will get you dramatically different results than what you experienced last time…. You do want to… sell your home this time… right? (*Yes.*)

And if I could help you… get full market value for it in the next 30 days… you said… that would not be a problem… right? (*Yes.*) Perfect.

When would be the best time for us to… get together… for me to share with you exactly how I do that….tomorrow at 4:15, or would 5:15 be better?

YESMaster Strategy: Whenever a seller's objection is designed to cut you off (like this one), repeat and affirm their answer as if it's just something they are considering. E.g. "So right now you're planning to re-list with the same agent…. Got it." Instead of, "Oh, you're going to re-list with the same agent… Got it." The difference is subtle, but significant.

"WHAT ARE YOU GOING TO DO DIFFERENTLY THAN THE OTHERS?"

Well...(with a chuckle) the main thing is... I'm going to... get it sold! That is what you want, right? (Yes.) Of course.

I am going to help you... get it done... in the best amount of time, with the least amount of hassle and...put the most money in your pocket ...possible in this market...and get you to ________________ ("your new home in LA...). Because ultimately that's what you want, right?

When would be the best time for us to... get together... for me to share with you how I will help you do that....tomorrow at 2:15, or would 4:15 be better?

"I HATE YOUR COMPANY."

Ugh..you gotta be kidding. [*With disgust...*] What happened? [*Let them rant.*]

Can I tell you something else? (What?) It's not the first time I've heard that...can you believe it? (Yes.)

So...here's the deal...IF you could... get your property sold for top dollar... in the next 30 days...is that something you still want to do? (Yes.) Excellent.

Look...I'm not going to defend an agent from our company who was unprofessional, but I'm NOT that agent...and you said you do still want to get the property sold, correct? (Yes.) Perfect.

And...if I could help you make that that happen...that would be okay with you, right? (Yes.) Great!

When would be a good time for us to... get together...tomorrow at 4:15, or would 5:15 be better?

YESMaster Strategy: The key here is to *be on their side*. The moment you try to defend your company, you become *the enemy*. If you have been with your company for any length of time, you have heard other negative stories about something an agent did. Your best chance is to agree with them and share their disgust that something like that could happen. It positions you as their ally, rather than as their adversary, so you can earn the opportunity to help them.

"I WISH YOU REALTORS WOULD JUST LEAVE ME ALONE!"

Ah… So you're getting hammered by real estate agents calling you, huh? ( ) Ugh...I understand how annoying that can be.

So let me just ask this… How much time will you take before you will… consider hiring a strong agent… for the job of selling your house...if...they could help you net the money you need in your pocket?

[*And then continue with the FSBO SCRIPT or EXPIRED SCRIPT.*]

"WHERE WERE YOU WHEN MY HOUSE WAS ON THE MARKET?"

That's a great question…and I hear where you're coming from…

The short answer is because your house wasn't a match for any of my buyers I was working with at the time…. However…can I let you know something else? (Yes.)

The reason I didn't have a buyer match for your home is because…unfortunately…my focus wasn't specifically on your property. And I say unfortunately…because…it sounds like you are really interested in getting your property sold, correct? (Yes.) Excellent.

If you knew you could… get the property sold… for top dollar in the next 30 days or so, would that be a win for you? (Yes.) Fantastic.

And if I could help you make that happen, that would be OK with you, right? (Yes.) Perfect!

When would be a good time for us to… get together… tomorrow at 4:15, or would 5:15 be better?

"WE'VE ALREADY CHOSEN AN AGENT." OR "WE'VE ALREADY SET ALL THE INTERVIEWS WE WANT."

[*Repeat and affirm the objection.*] I understand not wanting to parade a bunch of agents through...ugh...

What if...you knew you could have it sold for top dollar in less than 30 days... guaranteed? ...I assume that would not be a problem, correct? (No.) Good.

And you obviously don't want to... put it on the market again... to have it...NOT sell...right?" (No.) Great!

And if I could get you top dollar in 30 days or less, that would be OK with you, yes? (Yes.) Perfect...

And Look...I'm not going to waste your time...or mine. You're obviously a sharp guy/gal... and when we... get together... if you feel like our conversation isn't going anywhere (or you decide I'm full of B.S.) at any point...you simply say the word...and I'll leave...no pressure. We'll just shake hands and... be friends. Fair enough? Great.

YESMasters Strategy: Notice that you are **not** talking about **you** at all. It's all about what the seller wants: results and respect.

"YOU'RE THE 50TH REALTOR THAT'S CALLED TODAY!"

Ugh...so you're getting hammered by agents calling... Yeah...I understand how annoying that can be...

[*Then continue with the EXPIRED SCRIPT or FSBO SCRIPT.*]

YESMasters Strategy: The key is to ***mirror and match*** their frustration/irritation. If you try to be sympathetic or apologetic it only makes it worse. Be frustrated with them (not at them). And then go on with your script.

"WHAT WILL YOU DO THAT THE LAST AGENT DIDN'T... TO GET IT SOLD?"

That's a great question... I'm not sure exactly what they did... but obviously you don't want to... put it on the market again... to have it not sell, correct? (Of course.) Great.

So the first thing I will do is some homework on your house and a thorough market study to find out why it didn't sell... And what it's going to take to actually... get it sold... because again that's what you want, right? (Yes.) Excellent.

And then second... when we meet... I'll lay out exactly what I'm going to do to get you the result you're hiring me for... Fair enough? (Yes.) Perfect.

So...when you... get this property sold... where are you going next?

[*Go on with the EXPIRED SCRIPT questions #2 through #4 to clarify the sellers' motivation and then set up a time to meet.*]

YESMaster ANSWER - *If you have the track record to say it:*

You really want me to tell you over the phone?

I've listed ____ expireds in the last ____ months and SOLD **every one** of them for top dollar. Now, is that a result you could live with? (Yes.) Cool!

I'm going to do exactly the same thing for you that I did for them. Are you with me? (Yes.) Great!

[*OPTIONAL if you offer a guaranteed sale*] PLUS…when you…hire me…I will guarantee the results…or I'll pay you for me wasting your time. Fair enough? (Yes.) Perfect.

> This final "PLUS" answer applies only if you offer a Guaranteed Sale which I teach in detail in "Double Your Listing Power." Visit www.DoubleYourListingPower.com to find out more.

"WHY SHOULD I HIRE YOU?"

1. That is a great question. Here are the top 3 reasons that you would…want to hire me:

    1. Because I sell every listing…for top dollar.

    2. Because I guarantee my results….

    3. Because I care about what's important to you.

1. I assume you're interested in results, right? (Yes.) Perfect.
2. Then when would be a good time for us to… get together… I could come out today at 4:15 or tomorrow at 2:15… which would be better for you?

YESMaster Strategy: I know that a lot of real estate people would say this script is unrealistic, but that is because of the amateur approach most agents take toward sellers and listings. We allow sellers to "be the expert" or allow them to list the home at a price that it will not sell. That is not professional. That is amateur.

When you price a listing correctly, make sure it shows well and is easy to show, and market it properly, it will sell. An "ugly house" simply requires a price that compensates for the condition and the fact that is does not show well.

If you can't honestly use this script, it's time to improve your game. It's time to "Go pro" and "be a hero" …to your sellers and to yourself.

"WE'RE GOING TO LIST WITH THE AGENT THAT SOLD US THE HOUSE."

So…you're thinking about just using the agent that sold you the house. That makes sense.

Can I ask you a question? (Sure.) Which is more important to you…sticking with the agent who helped you buy the house…or…getting the best results in the sale of your property? (Results.) Good for you!

[OPTIONAL]: By best results…I mean…getting the most money, in the best time, with the smoothest process. In other words…is this a friendship decision…or a business decision?

And…they could be the best agent for you…so…I'm not necessarily saying you should…switch agents… and… hire me to do the job for you. What I'm suggesting is that you at least… take a look at an option… that could get you a better result. Are you with me…about the idea of getting *you* the best results? (Yes.) Excellent.

When would be the best time to get together and… go over some options… that will help you get the best results possible…I could come out tomorrow at 2:15…or would 4:15 be better?

YESMaster Strategy: You never win by dogging the other agent. Focus on what the seller wants which is to get the house sold. That's what this script does. It helps shift the focus from the agent to the result they want.

"WE'RE GOING WITH X-COMPANY BECAUSE THEY ARE THE #1 OFFICE IN THE AREA."

I hear you...and having a company with market share can definitely be an advantage! And can I let you know something else? (Yes.)

I'm sure you realize that when you're looking at large offices and agents, that ultimately it isn't the company you are hiring, but the individual agent, right? (Yes.)

Think about it this way… and this is something a lot of people are not aware of… often the largest company also has the highest number of brand new agents...and almost every company has agents that sell a lot of homes and agents that sell very few or even NO homes at all! Make sense? (Yes.)

So I guess the question is, what is the best way to… make sure you don't get stuck with the wrong agent… even in a good company? Are you with me? (Yes.)

Is the size of the company most important, or hiring the right agent that will give (guarantee) you the best results? (Right agent.) Absolutely.

That's what I do… And if I could help you… get your property sold… for top dollar in the best amount of time for you…that would be OK with you, right? (Sure.) Perfect!

Then when would be a good time for us to… get together… I could come out tomorrow at 2:15…or would 4:15 be better?

LISTING APPOINTMENT SELLER OBJECTIONS

A DECISION-MAKER NO-SHOW: "MY SPOUSE COULDN'T MAKE IT…."

Let's do this….when would be a better time for us to meet when both of you can… be here? ….I can either come back in an hour or would tomorrow at 6:15 be better?

Seller: That's OK… You can just show me… and then I'll talk it over with my husband/wife.

I appreciate that. And…I'd like to be able to do that….however, it's very important that all of us be able to meet…..since obviously….I am going to be working for both of you….right?

That way we can… make sure… we're all on the same page…and….so that I can answer both of your questions…. Does that make sense?

Plus…(chuckle) I want to make sure…we all like each other…since we are going to be working together…right?

So will tomorrow at 6:15 work….or would tomorrow at 6:45 be better?

> **YESMaster Strategy:** First, do not be irritated or make the Sellers wrong when one of them no-shows. Second, clarify why one of the decision makers is unavailable.

"WHAT ARE YOU GOING TO DO TO MARKET MY HOME?"

That's a great question.

[Optional]) Did you have a chance to look over the Action Plan in the information package I sent over yesterday? ( ) Excellent/No problem. Basically it says...

I am going to do everything it takes to... get your home exposed... to ALL of the qualified buyers in the market... [NODDING] which is the kind of buyers you want looking at your house, correct? (*Yes.*) Great!

That's my job. That's what my action plan does.

The important thing today is that we... price your home accurately... so that when we get the qualified buyers in here, they'll be excited about buying your home versus the competition...because again... [NODDING] that is the result we want, right? (*Yes.*) Exactly!

And if we don't... price it correctly... no amount of marketing will help. Does that make sense? (*Yes.*) Perfect.

YESMaster Strategy: Body Language is even more powerful than your words! So make sure when you are asking questions for a "yes" that your face is pleasant and your head is nodding up and down affirming the right answer.

Remember, this answer is designed to be used only at the listing presentation.

If they ask this question before the listing presentation, your answer is: "That's a great question, and obviously that is something we'll go over when we meet."

If they say, "Just email it to me," or 'Just tell me over the phone." Your answer is: "Sure. In fact, as soon as we... schedule a time to meet, I'm going to send you an entire packet of information including my action plan to...get your home sold. Sound great?" This is your pre-listing packet.

"WE'RE LOOKING FOR SOME REALLY AGGRESSIVE MARKETING TO GET BUYERS IN HERE WHO WILL PAY WHAT OUR HOUSE IS WORTH."

Absolutely...Because the key is getting qualified, motivated buyers into your house, right? (Of course.) Exactly.

And… that is what my action plan does. Just to clarify…I'm sure you… understand …that marketing does not make your house worth more. Does that make sense? Obviously…buyers are not comparing the marketing strategies…right?

They are comparing your home…with the other homes on the market… And when they're looking at 2 or 3 similar homes…what is the number one thing they are comparing? (*Price.*) Exactly.

So the key today…is to make sure we… price your home accurately… so that when we get the qualified buyers in here, they'll be excited about buying your home versus the competition… because again… [*NODDING*] that is the result we want, right? (*Yes.*) Exactly!

And if we don't… price it correctly… no amount of marketing will help. Does that make sense? (*Yes.*) Perfect.

YESMaster Strategy: Notice that you are always agreeing with the seller's perspective, even if their thinking is inaccurate. You are NOT agreeing in this case with their belief, but you are agreeing with what they want to accomplish. Then you can gently correct their inaccurate thinking without creating resistance.

"WE'RE LOOKING FOR SOMEONE WHO'S GOING TO FALL IN LOVE WITH OUR HOUSE AND BE WILLING TO PAY OUR PRICE."

I understand what you mean. ...because when you found this home...you absolutely fell in love with it... right? (Yes.) Exactly.

So... how much above full market value did you pay when you bought it? (*We didn't pay above market value.*) So...If the sellers had asked you to pay an extra $50,000 [*USE A NUMBER THAT IS ABOUT 10% OF THE HOUSE'S VALUE*] would you have paid $50,000 above current market value...even if you loved it? (*Of course not.*) Exactly!

See...you want someone who will fall in love with your house, right? ( ) Because that is the buyer who will pay the most for it...make sense? (*Yes*) Exactly.

Can I tell you the irony? (*Yes.*) Pricing it high will actually KEEP buyers from falling in love with your house... can I explain? (*Yes.*)

And this is why it's important to... understand the Buyer's perspective. ...Because what they see BEFORE they see the house....is the price....and because it's higher than the competition... the price actually makes them afraid to fall in love with it. So... they actually come see your home...trying NOT to fall in love with it...just because of the price. [PAUSE] Are you beginning to see why I'm concerned about pricing it high?

"WE'RE NOT INTERESTED IN JUST TAKING THE FIRST OFFER THAT COMES ALONG. WE'RE WILLING TO WAIT LONGER IF WE NEED TO...TO GET OUR PRICE."

Sure…you want to make sure that the offer you accept is in fact the best offer, right? (*Of course.*) That makes sense.

Can I share with you something many sellers and even a lot of agents are not aware of? (*Yes.*) That statistically the best offer received on a property is almost always the first one… regardless of how long a property takes to sell. Isn't that interesting? ( ) Yes.

And here is the even more shocking truth… sellers who list their homes over-priced actually end up selling for less…because they sit on the market too long and become stagnant. And then…after weeks and weeks on the market the "W.W.W.T.H. Syndrome" kicks in… "What's Wrong With That House." You obviously don't want that to end up happening, right? (*No*) Exactly.

There is one exception to the "First Offer Rule" …and that is if we get multiple offers…which can get you the highest price of all! That would be OK with you… right? The only way to make that possible is to make sure we… price it competitively. Does that make sense? (Yes.) Excellent!

"SINCE WE'RE LOSING MONEY/HAVING TO REDUCE OUR PRICE...WILL YOU ALSO REDUCE YOUR COMMISSION?"

That's a fair question...and the reality is...I've already cut my commission...because the fact that you're having to... sell your home... for a lower price means my commission is automatically reduced, because my commission is tied directly to the sales price, right? (Yes.) Exactly.

So just like you...I'm taking a big cut in how much money I get too. Make sense? ( ) Good.

[*OPTIONAL depending on your current market*] And even worse is that selling a house today is significantly more work now than it used to be. So I have to work harder and *still* make less money. So...as you can see...the reality is that you and I are both hit by what the market is telling us about the value of your house. See what I mean? (Yes) Terrific!

The key is that I'm going to do everything possible to still get the best price and terms for you that's possible in this market. Fair enough? (Yes.) Excellent.

"WILL YOU CUT YOUR COMMISSION?"

That is a great question. Discounting commissions is not something I do. Can I tell you why? (Yes.) BECAUSE…I don't deliver discount results.

[*OPTIONAL*] There's already too many agents out there who don't get half their listings sold...who don't deliver results. And that's obviously NOT what you're looking for, is it? (No.) Good.

I assume you do… want the best results, right? (Yes/Well…) I hear you!

And the best results means the most money possible in your pocket...in the best amount of time…with the least hassle… Are you with me on getting you the best results? (Yes.) Excellent!

BECAUSE…that's what we both want…yes? (Yes.) Exactly.

So…here's what I'm going to do for you… As soon as you… give me the go ahead… I'm going to go to work immediately to make that happen for you. Sound good? (Yes.) Perfect!

YESMaster Strategy: Never answer this question with a "No." That word is one of the most powerful resistance triggers in the English language. Nobody likes to be told "No."

This script gives them a valid and compelling reason why you don't reduce your commission without making them feel turned down. Never be apologetic or tentative when discussing commission. After all, you work for free until you deliver results.

"HOW OFTEN WILL OUR HOME BE ADVERTISED IN THE NEWSPAPER/PRINT ADVERTISING?"

That's a great question. We actually do not use newspaper/print advertising anymore. And...that used to be an important marketing strategy back in the 1900s, but not today. Can I explain why? (*Yes.*)

Simply because newspapers/printed publications are not where serious buyers go to find homes for sale anymore...for a lot of reasons. #1) The information is out of date by the time it's printed, plus #2) the amount of information is too limited, and #3) they can't sort through it efficiently like they can on the internet. Does that make sense? (*Yes.*) Terrific.

[OPTIONAL] Not to mention...killing more trees using outdated advertising methods isn't friendly to our environment....is it? (No.) Exactly.

The most important thing is that we... get your home exposed... to where the qualified buyers are looking, right? (*Right.*)

Because what you're wanting is to find the best buyer for your house, correct? (*Yes.*) That's what my Action Plan will do for you.

So, do you have any more questions...or are you ready to... put me to work for you? (*Ready.*) Perfect!

YESMaster Strategy: This approach is what I call the "Hot-Potato" Technique. The principle is this: the one asking the questions in the one in control of the conversation. When they toss a "hot-potato" question at you and you answer it, they are in total control. When you answer the question and then immediately follow it with a question that leads the conversation in the direction you want it to go, you are now back in control. Every time you ask a question, you are figuratively tossing them a "hot-potato" that they have to deal with.

In some real estate markets, especially in the luxury markets, there is still a number of real estate advertising magazines and books in print that you may have to deal with this issue. Newspaper advertising is becoming less and less common, but the answer is the same for any print media advertising.

"WE'LL SAVE THE COMMISSION BY SELLING IT OURSELVES."

FSBO APPROACH #1:

1. It's true...you could avoid the commission by selling it yourself…but are you aware that generally less than 10% of all For Sale By Owners actually sell on their own? (No.)
2. Most of them will eventually… hire an agent… to actually… get the property sold. And what's more alarming is that generally up to 50% of contracts of people selling the house themselves don't even close! Did you know that? (No)
3. Can I explain why that happens? (Yes.) Because many of these buyers either are not qualified or...they don't do what it takes to get financing because they simply don't know what to do. And in today's market… getting a loan is infinitely more difficult today than in the past… I'm sure you're aware of that, right? (yes) Exactly.
4. And then, after that deal falls apart, the sellers have already bought or rented their next house, and end up having to… list the house with a Realtor anyway... or they take less for it to make it… sell fast… and avoid double mortgage payments…plus the extra cost and liability of having a vacant home. Obviously, you don't want that to happen, right? (Right) Good.
5. Would you prefer more risk...or less risk? (Less.) Of course.

6. I will help you dramatically… reduce your risks… that come with the Do-it-yourself approach. Won't that be nice? (Yes) Excellent.

FSBO APPROACH #2

1. It is possible for a person to sell themselves…[chuckle] I could also cut my own hair, right? (Yes) Of course...but the reason most people are willing to… pay for a professional service… is that they realize that the value of the service they get is worth additional investment, right? (yes) Exactly.
2. Here's what most For Sale By Owners that… hire me…discover: They make as much or **more** money by deciding to… let me handle it. ...**And** they also... avoid all the stress and hassle… and **risk** of costly "do-it-yourself" mistakes. Doesn't that make sense? (yes) Perfect.
3. And by now...you're probably beginning to realize that most buyers who shop For-Sale-By-Owners are either...looking for owner-financing *because they're not qualified*…or they're bargain-hunters *wanting a steal* since there are no commissions, right? ( ) Have you already seen that happening? (Yes) Ouch.
4. So you end up wasting your time with unqualified buyers, or you end up giving the commission to the buyer and you still have to do all the work yourself…plus all the risk and legal liability. Does that make sense? (Yes) Excellent!

LEADING FSBO TO THE "YES."

1. Is the commission your biggest concern…or is it really the bottom line that's most important to you? (Bottom line) Good.

2. Usually, I can net you the same amount or more in your pocket at closing…as you can. Wouldn't that be great? (Of course.) Excellent!
3. I'll do all the work…and it really costs you nothing, right? (Yes.) Great!

FSBO MOTIVATED BUYER SCENARIO:

Let's say I'm a qualified, serious buyer. Which is what you're looking for, correct? (Yes.) Great! I need to buy a house this week….ok? I have two options:

Number one...I can go to Craigslist or search the internet, find some FSBO's, and then use my own car, my own gas, and my own time and energy and go look at a very limited selection of houses, not really knowing what I'm going to find when I get there. And then do all the work myself…and hope I find a house I like...

Or number two...I can find a professional buyer's agent to get a full selection of available properties on the market….use their car, their gas, their expertise, and their knowledge of the market to find the perfect house at a fair price without the hassle. …And you know what? (What?) ….That's what almost all motivated, qualified buyers do. Does that make sense? (Yes) Good.

Wouldn't it be nice to...let me help you...get motivated, qualified buyers...in your house this weekend? (Yes) Absolutely.

ASK FOR THE DECISION

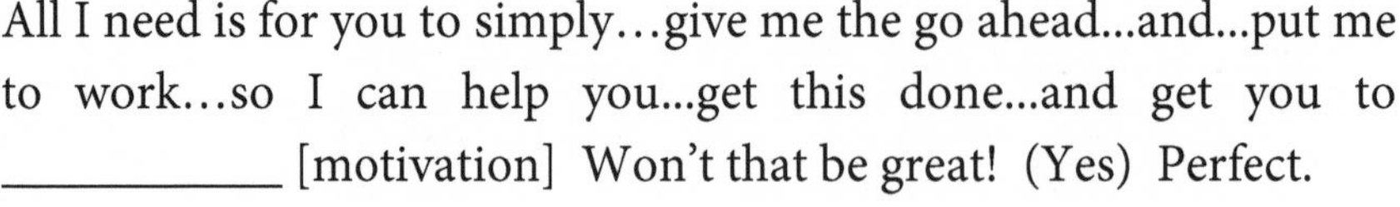
All I need is for you to simply…give me the go ahead...and...put me to work…so I can help you...get this done...and get you to ____________ [motivation] Won't that be great! (Yes) Perfect.

"WE NEED TO THINK ABOUT IT..." - THE DEDUCTION APPROACH

Obviously… This is a big decision, isn't it? Just so I'm clear, and to make sure I haven't missed anything that you need to…make a decision, let's…clarify specifically...what still needs thinking about….

Because…usually there's really three major issues to decide:

#1 is whether or not you're actually going to... sell your property, right? Do you need to think about that… or is that decision already made?

#2 is what price are we going to... list your property…for, right? (Yes.) And it seems like we're pretty well in agreement on what price it needs to be listed at…correct? (Yes.)

> [*OPTIONAL*] Even though it's obviously less than you want…you can… see why that is the right price, correct? ( ) I don't like it either! I would love to be able to get you $_____ for your home. Unfortunately, that's not what the market is telling us…does that make sense?
>
> And "thinking about it" is not going to change the reality of the market, right?

So…is there anything about the pricing that you still need time to think about? (I guess not.) Great.

And #3 is simply to... decide... if... I am the agent you want to hire...because you... feel confident... that I will get the job done for you and get you the best results. Because results are what counts, right? (Yes.) Excellent! Do you... feel confident about that? (Yes.) Perfect.

[*OPTIONAL*] Is there anything you think is important that's missing...or that I've not covered? ...or that you don't... feel comfortable... with? [*If there is...now you can handle it.*]

Then it sounds like we're ready to... get started... agreed? (Yes.) [*Extend hand.*] Congratulations!

YESMaster Strategy: Any time a prospect tells you "We need to think about it," there is something they are not telling you. This objection is a smoke screen for their real concern, so if you leave at this point without a decision, your chances of getting the listing are very slim.

The Deduction Approach works so beautifully because it breaks down and simplifies the decision-making process for them. And when they feel confident in you as a professional and they are motivated to sell, this process will either draw out the real objection so you can address it, or it will help lead them to go ahead and simply make the decision to hire you.

As you master the conversations in this book, you will find your confidence increasing dramatically and the way sellers respond to your confidence will amaze you. You win and they win. YES!

YOUR NEXT STEP

I make one promise to my coaching members: "***When you work with me and master what I teach you to do, people will not be able to tell you 'no.'"*** They won't *want* to tell you "no." When you show up as a true professional with a commitment to their best interest, you make people feel safe and want to hire you and to work only with you.

This book has given you the play book…the tools…to begin having that kind of influence and effectiveness with people. An amateur will take this and give it a try using the good ole D-I-Y approach…and with enough effort they will get some listings and make some money. Which is great. But if you are interested in mastery…in going PRO…I know you know you need more.

Those are the kinds of agents that choose to work with me. What happens with agents who go through my training is you began to master the strategies and skills in a way that will 3X, 5X, or even 10X your business. It doesn't happen overnight, but two years from now, you will not even recognize your business or your bank account because there will be so much money in it!

If that is the kind of results you want and you are committed to it, you should at least make sure you have taken advantage of all the complimentary BONUS TRAINING AND RESOURCE you received with **The Book of "YES,"** by visiting www.thebookofyes.com/bonuses.

Study it. Practice it. Implement it. Master it.

ABOUT THE AUTHOR: KEVIN WARD

Kevin Ward is the founder of YESMasters Real Estate Success Training, one of the fastest growing and most comprehensive training programs for real estate agents in the world.

Kevin has trained tens of thousands of real estate agents, and his online training videos are watched on YouTube by thousands of real estate agents every week. He is known internationally for his high-powered yet practical, real-world strategies and for his ability to make skills and scripts simple and learnable for agents at every level. The 10X power of Kevin's Real Estate Vortex system and his "NO-BS" approach to real estate sales are quickly becoming legendary.

Before getting into real estate, Kevin grew up as a shy country boy from West Texas who lived in a mobile home on a small farm with his parents, sister, a stray dog named Chiquita, 2 or 3 cats, a few chickens and pigs, and his uncle's cows. Kevin says, "As a teenager, I was so shy…I would way rather talk to our farm animals than to people."

When Kevin began selling real estate, he had just moved from a small town to the DFW Metroplex with no savings, no connections, and no previous real estate or sales experience. Kevin recalls, "I had never even owned my own house! I was terrified, but determined…and so I jumped into real estate with both feet. The first time I knocked on a FSBO's door, he yelled at me to "get the f**k off my porch!" I was so traumatized I wouldn't knock on another door for over a year." In spite of his "near-death" experience, Kevin adjusted and kept on prospecting (mostly by phone) and by his 3rd year, he sold over 100 homes in one year.

Kevin launched YesMasters Real Estate Success Training, not only to provide the highest quality training, but also to create a community of real estate professionals who are committed to a "No-BS approach" to real estate, and to getting "more YES's and more successes in their business...*and in their life.*"

Kevin lives with his wife, Julie, in Las Vegas with their Beagle, Homie, and their rescued cat (who believes he is royalty), Elvis. They also enjoy spending time at the beach at their second home in Los Angeles. Kevin says he is a teacher at heart, maybe because both of his parents were teachers. He has his Bachelor's degree in Education from Abilene Christian University and his Master of Arts degree in Communication and Ministry from Oklahoma Christian University of Science and Arts. He loves reading, traveling, sailing, basketball, and watching breathtaking sunsets with his wife.

KEVIN'S COACHING PROGRAMS

MASTERY COACHING: LIVE weekly coaching calls and role play calls with Kevin Ward in an interactive conference call format with personal on-demand video coaching and much more…

THE 100-DAY LISTMASTER CHALLENGE: An intense 100-day coaching program personally led by Kevin Ward and designed to transform your business and your life through accelerated learning and implementation of strategies, skills, systems, and success mindset with high levels of support and accountability.

KEVIN'S INNER CIRCLE & MASTERMIND: Elite weekly coaching with Kevin Ward for agents who are making $200,000+ or closing 36+ transactions a year. (Must have successfully completed The 100-Day ListMaster Challenge to qualify for the Inner Circle).

THE BEST: Kevin's Private 1-on-1 Mentorship Program. Must be qualified for the Inner Circle. By invitation only.

NOTE: Because Kevin is your coach and does not "outsource" you to other coaches, registration into Kevin's coaching programs is extremely limited.

To see all of Kevin's Coaching Programs, please visit:

www.YESMasters.com/coaching

KEVIN'S ONLINE PROGRAMS AND LIVE TRAINING CAMPS

Double Your Listing Power Online Training and 3-Day Training Camp: "The Best Listing Agent Training in the World." Kevin Ward has combined the most cutting-edge, high-profit strategies, influence and communication skills training, and business systems training to help you get more listings, get better results, have more control of your time, make more money...and actually have a LIFE during the process. Experience the most advanced, comprehensive, and innovative listing agent training available anywhere...GUARANTEED.

FX Extreme Online Training and Intensive 3-Day Training Camp on Listing and Selling FSBO's and Expireds: The best and most comprehensive training in the world on how to list and sell high volumes of For-Sale-By-Owners and Expireds. Whether you are brand new or a seasoned FSBO/Expired "Ninja," this mastery course will dramatically increase your effectiveness and results.

The Real Estate Vortex Online Training and 3-Day Training Camp: Build a 7-Figure Business by Leveraging the Power of Relationships. Using simple yet powerful systems and revolutionary frameworks, Kevin has created the ultimate Step-by-Step, No-BS, Fast-Track System for realistically and profitably doing hundreds of deals a year while having the lifestyle you deserve. Build a Word-of-Mouth Marketing Team that brings you a constant flow of business. And leverage your success to create financial freedom in 5 to 10 years.

Ultimate Objection Mastery: Lifetime access to the ultimate online video training program for overcoming objections that delivers game-changing results, more appointments and more listings! GUARANTEED! Learn killer objection-handlers for the 10 toughest objections agents face with sellers, along with "deep-dive" training videos to guide you in mastering your delivery of each objection-handler. Includes additional bonus objection-handlers and video and audio training.

Agent Power Launch: A comprehensive online training course for new and rookie real estate agents, that gives you the step-by-step tactical instructions for how to create a profitable and sustainable real estate business fast. You get lifetime access to 12 in-depth modules plus hours of bonus video and audio training. Learn the best strategies, skills, systems, and success mindset for launching and building a successful real estate career.

To see all of Kevin's training programs, please visit:

www.YESMasters.com/training

ACKNOWLEDGEMENTS

No one succeeds alone, and I know that. Since my first day as a new, terrified real estate agent, I have been fortunate to have many great mentors and coaches through the years who trained me and supported my success.

All the scripts that I have created and used and taught have been tremendously influenced by people who have been my real estate mentors and coaches through the years. I would like to express special appreciation to the following:

To Mike Bowman, my first broker at Century 21 Mike Bowman, who taught me that listings were the name of the game. Mike, leaving your company for "greener pastures" was the first huge business mistake I made in real estate. To Dan Gault, I could not have asked for a better trainer as a new agent. You got me to talk to strangers even though I didn't want to and wouldn't take any excuses. To Dave Bowman, you are are a tribute to leadership in our industry and a great manager and broker who models no B.S. To Jeane Dees, you showed me the power of straightforward conversation and you always had my back. You are one of the best! Thank you.

To Floyd Wickman, the creator of Sweat Hogs…I am one! To Mike Ferry, you are "The Godfather" of real estate coaching, period. To John Furber, who was my first one-on-one coach, you helped me get to that magical 100 deals in one year. To Ken Goodfellow, you taught me the importance of really knowing my numbers. To Neil Schwartz, a true "Super-broker," trainer, coach, and owner of Century 21 Masters, who understands the importance of practice and mastering scripts, and his agents' success proves it. I learned so much from you even beyond real estate.

I want to thank my mom and dad for their lifelong support for me. Mom, I miss you. Dad, thank you for your valuable suggestions and editorial help in preparing this book. To Mary Anglin, thank you for editing this book (twice!) and proving to be an amazingly good editor. I'm proud to have you as a coaching members and for your courage to stand up to resistance.

To Adam Markel and Peak Potentials' Quantum Leap, you helped me discover my power and have the courage to fight for my dreams. To T. Harv Eker, the creator of Millionaire Mind Intensive, that was the weekend I decided to go after my life's dream and my mission one more time.

To Tony Robbins' Unleash the Power Within 2012 in Los Angeles for teaching me I could walk on fire and inspiring me to take action.

To Alex Mandossian, your Ultimate Internet Boot Camp showed my how to build a website from scratch, get my message online, and how to actually make money with it. Two months later I launched what would become YesMasters Real Estate Success Training.

To Brendon Burchard, you gave me the vision and belief that my message was valuable. Before I could even afford to come to any of your events, your free videos and your commitment to adding value became the model for my entire business.

To James Malinchak, when I first hired you to coach me, I barely had enough money to pay for the first month! You immediately gave me clarity and amazing strategies that helped me turn

YesMasters into a business that actually started making me money…and making a greater impact for others.

To Elena Pezzini, thank you for all the suggestions and coaching and support and for your friendship to Julie and me.

To Austin Netzley and his team at Epic Launch, thank you for helping turn the vision of this book into a reality.

To Mel Abraham, thanks for your generous input on publishing my first book, for your mentorship, encouragement, and mostly for your friendship. Everyone should hope to someday have a friend like you.

To Greg Hague, you blow my mind with your maverick strategies that actually work with no B.S., and that you have proven with your own massive success. Thank you for being one of my biggest supporters and encouragers and for being a true friends without reservation. You are rare air, my friend.

To Tim Adams, thank you for kicking my butt, for teaching me how to move, and for making me powerful on stage and off.

To Roger Love, the greatest vocal coach in the world, you have given my voice true power and helped me not to lose it any more. Even after all the famous people you have coached, you have one of the most caring hearts I have ever seen. I'm honored to count you as one of my friends.

To Bo Eason, you have had a greater impact in my life than anyone other than my father, because it was you who gave me permission to be THE BEST. You showed me how huge my responsibility is, and helped me understand the real work required to become the BEST.

To my Inner Circle MasterMind coaching members…you guys are the BEST. I love working with you and watching your successes.

To my 100-Day ListMaster Challenge graduates, and all my Mastery Coaching members for proving the effectiveness of these scripts and the power of "YesMastery." You are raising the bar in the industry. Thank you.

And finally to Julie, thank you for suggesting we go skydiving five years ago. The day we jumped out of that plane together I knew that fear would never stop me again. If someone ever had a muse...you are mine. I love you.

ONE LAST THING...

If **The Book of "YES"** has inspired or helped you, would you *let me know?* Email your success stories to me personally at kevin@Yesmasters.com.

And help me spread the word. The public is fed up with B.S. sales approaches, and agents are tired of feeling like they have to use it to succeed. Help me get the word out that you can get "yes" without the B.S.

Give a copy to your broker or sales manager. Tell other agents about it. Together we can reset the bar of integrity and professionalism, and raise the level of respect in this amazing real estate industry. *Thanks for making a difference!*

I look forward to meeting you at one of my training camps soon and shaking your hand and hearing personally about your wins.

YES!
Kevin Ward